Rainstorm of Tomorrow
The Ever-Flowing Banquet of Philosophy

Renyuan Dong

Copyright 2020 by MSI Press, LLC

All rights reserved. No part of this book may be reproduced or utilized in any form or by any means, electronic or mechanical, including photocopying, recording, or by any information storage and retrieval system, without permission in writing from the publisher.

For information, contact
MSI Press
1760-F Airline Highway, #203
Hollister, CA 95023

Cover graphic by Inna Bigun/Shutterstock
Cover design by Carl D. Leaver
Copyedited by Mary Ann Raemisch

Permission for image reproductions granted by Association Marcel Duchamp/ADAGP, David Hammons/Tilton Gallery, Dreamstime, El Anatsui/Jack Shainman Gallery, Fundació Gala-Salvador Dalí, Japanese Society for Protecting Artists' Rights (JASPAR), ProLitteris, Scala Archives (representative for the Museum of Modern Art), SHUEISHA Inc., Shutterstock.

Permission for text reproductions granted by Nmlongyou (TikTok Vlogger).

Library of Congress Control Number 2020901727

ISBN: 9781950328192

Contents

Acknowledgments v

Preface 1

Part One
Truth 7

Chapter 1. **Tree Growing into the Soil with Its Roots Buried in the Air** . . 9
Core Question: Is the world of nature knowable?

Chapter 2. **The World As a Fundamentally Material Being** 15
Core Question: Is the reality of the world material or mental? Or both?

Chapter 3. **All Questions Are Involved with Logos** 25
*Core Question: What language should we use
to describe the material nature of the world?*

Chapter 4. **Quantum Theory and the Ultimate Aim of Science** 41
*Core Question: Is the purpose of science purely to seek truth
or to guide practice?*

Epilogue 1. **Distant Similarity and Astonishing Conjecture** 53
Core Question: What is the essential structure of the universe?

Part Two
Ethics 67

Chapter 5. **Survival and Reproduction—
Another Language for Utilitarianism** 69
Core Question: What Is the Meaning of Life?

Chapter 6. **Is Happiness More Important Than Anything Else in Life?** . 79
*Core Question: What are the Similarities and Differences
between Utilitarianism and Hedonism?*

Chapter 7. **The Conformity to Utilitarianism by Anti-Utilitarian Events
and the Violation of Utilitarianism by Utilitarian Events** . . 89
*Core Question: How is the Unity of Opposites
Demonstrated in Utilitarianism?*

Chapter 8. **The Corralled "Free Will"** 101
Core Question: Does Utilitarianism Overthrow Free Will?

Chapter 9. **Sunday Mass Unattended by God** 109
    *Core Question: Will the Human Species Evolve
into Superman or even into God?*

Epilogue 2. **To the Masses As Well As to the Mavericks** 117
    *Core Question: Systematic Value Conflicts—How to Deal
with the Conflict between Pursuit for Self and Social Demands?*

Part Three
Aesthetics 127

Chapter 10. **Beauty Skin Deep and Beauty to the Bone** 129
    Core Question: What is Beauty?

Chapter 11. **At the End of What You Should Know Is the
Beginning of What You Should Sense** 147
    Core Question: What is Art?

Chapter 12. **The Thousand-Faceted Aphrodite** 161
    *Core Question: Is There a Standard Aesthetic Paradigm
Guaranteeing the Beauty of Artworks in Accordance with It?*

Works Cited 173

Other Resources... 177

Acknowledgments

The author gives special thanks to Editage, a division of Cactus Communications as well as John Trujillo for English-language editing.

The author also thanks Connie Rogers Tilton of Tilton Gallery, Jack Shainman Gallery, and SHUEISHA Inc. for consultation and assistance with securing permissions for use of copyrighted materials.

Renyuan Dong

Preface

"Philosophy is dead," declared Stephen Hawking in agreement with many others. "As philosophers have not kept up with science, their art is dated" (Warman, 2011, n.p.). However, if we refer to the history of how humans persue knowledge, we will not find that different disciplines replaced one another in sequence. It is not that the wilt of religion gave rise to philosophy, or that the denouement of philosophy set the stage for science—nor is the world segmented into discrete, incompatible disciplinary fields. A biological reaction can be expanded to millions of chemical reactions or trillions of interactions between physical particles; likewise, the emergence of "social behaviors" among neural networks as they grow and that of "tacit agreement" from quantum entanglement have implied the possibility of adopting a sociological language to explain phenomena previously deemed as lifeless and strictly adherent to the laws of physics. Every discipline is a language capable of encompassing all phenomena in the world. Each speaks with a unique voice. In practice, however, we rarely lean on one discipline alone to explain everything around us. For example, we are not likely to use the language of physics—despite its sufficiency—to restore psychological activities to the interminable and trivial interactions of physical particles, on account of its low efficiency and incapacity to provide us with a holistic view. With the advancement of disciplinary differentiation, individual pieces of knowledge are often restrained to the little patch of his/her own specialty. For one to grasp the world in an all-encompassing picture, we need to weave the threads of different disciplines together; that tapestry is called the philosophy of science.

Rainstorm of Tomorrow: The Ever-Flowing Banquet of Philosophy is a book that dexterously weaves the storied philosophical themes of *truth*, *ethics*, and *aesthetics* together with the theories of relativity, quantum mechanics, neuroscience, epigenetics, social Darwinism, utilitarianism, evolutionary psychology, and modern art—from the soberest rationality to the wildest conjecture—to generate provocative or even alienating discourse on topics that you might otherwise regard yourself as being familiar with, and challenge you to re-think any settled positions that you may take for granted.

Part One, Truth, begins with an intriguing, playful metaphor—the tree growing into the soil with its roots buried in the air—to approach a subject that might otherwise have seemed too abstract or philosophical: the knowability of the world of nature. Does such a reversed perspective of the tree defy the existence of the world-in-itself in a manner akin to the counterintuitive theories advanced by quantum mechanics? If not, then how does the mirrored image challenge the language we use to describe the objective nature of the world? The chapters in Part One cope with these questions by scrutinizing the relationship between body and mind—also called matter and energy nowadays—as being simply the head and tail of the same coin. Further recruiting the theory of relativity, Part One ends by presenting the astonishing similarities across distant spatial and temporal scales and proposing the possibility of the universe as the inner cavity of a giant creature—as opposed to its stereotypical consideration as infinite and boundless. This take on truth imparts an almost mystical sense of what it is to be human, to be in this world, and to be conscious of the many ways we can apprehend it.

Part Two, Ethics, conceives of the ultimate meaning of present human existence as ensuring its continuation into the future: namely, *existence for existence's sake*. It interprets utilitarianism as a tool to achieve this goal in a biological language—as the drive underlying instinctive behaviors, including survival and reproduction. The chapters in this part, then, elaborate upon the complicated manifestation of utilitarianism, represented by the deceptively simple principle of "gaining advantage and avoiding harm," which is demonstrated by the conformity to utilitarianism by anti-utilitarian events and the violation of utilitarianism by seemingly utilitarian events. Through an eclectic selection of material from philosophy, psychology, genetic engineering, Chinese fables, Japanese anime, and Western dystopian novels, Part Two provides a multi-faceted, cross-cultural examination of what leading a "perfect" life means as well as how the possibilities for doing so will change in the future and what inherent tensions exist between self-fulfillment and social engagement. While addressing these questions, Part Two does not hesitate to broach controversial issues, such as whether humans will eventually evolve into immortals or ascend the throne of God.

Part Three, Aesthetics, probes the essence of beauty, art, and the existence of a standard aesthetic paradigm. It begins by describing many claptrap renditions of a tree, an object already familiar to you, and explains why such eye broccoli as analogs of modern art are more likely to be regarded as purely aesthetic objects than others exhibiting exterior beauty by stressing the transcendence of the utilitarian interest of aesthetics. The opposite of beauty is not ugliness but rather indifference and the cessation of work when the creation itself has no utilitarian purpose. The chapters in this part further speculate as to why preferences for some aesthetic concepts are universal while others may vary from person to person. Evolutionary psychology ascribes the establishment of universal aesthetic concepts to conflicts of interest in primitive human society, the origin of which having been long forgotten across centuries of memory inheritance. Memory is inheritable through our "encephalic waterpipes," made of semi-plastic, shape-memory alloys, which are gradually bent into different shapes under the continuous scouring of the everchanging environment and consequently generate diverse aesthetic paradigms. However, in the case of life-and-death, these flexible waterpipes will be restored to their original shape, manufactured from the same old mold, ensuring that any human is capable of employing an adequate stress reaction in response to threatening circumstances. Such conditioned reflexes are carved bone-deep into our memories in the form of beauty.

Overall, this volume casts light on philosophical questions that are described in scientific contexts but are ultimately beyond the reach of science—the type of questions that can be addressed but not answered so long as we hold to our position as human beings. That being said, philosophy remains one of the most frustrating disciplines in that it welcomes questions but evades answers. This never-perishing sense of frustration is symbolized by the book title, the everlasting *Rainstorm of Tomorrow*, which is not something to eliminate but rather to hail as the ultimate driver of human civilization.

The way that human civilization advances is sometimes described as the Red Queen's race. In a room that is constantly rolling backward, "it takes all the running you can do, to keep in the same place" (Carroll, 1993, p. 161). Many implications can be derived from this metaphor. First, how did this ecosystem come into being? Did the Red Queen enchant the ground to roll back first and then shut all kinds of species into the room in a nightmarish game of survival? Or was the initially static room set in motion by the disarrayed species themselves, with those unlucky enough to have run obliquely or opposite to the mainstream direction digging their own graves? In other words, did our ecosystem evolve into its present form spontaneously without any initial push or design? Human scientists are trying to unveil the origin of our evolution by exploring the necessary conditions that trigger artificial intelligence (AI).

Moreover, how fast can human beings evolve? The answer is the average backward speed of the room. While humans, as a front runner, have been accelerating the rotating speed and bringing those who can barely keep up with the pace to the brink of extinction, our evolutionary speed is also encumbered by the slower footpaces of other species, since the average speed of the room depends on all. Why do we choose to stay inside the room then? This is because we, as humans, share a symbiotic but non-identical interest with the *will-to-live*, a term frequently mentioned in Part Two, Ethics. While the *will-to-live* treats us with happiness in the form of social recognition whenever our ability increases, it ultimately aggregates individual achievements into collective progress that advances the continuous evolution of mankind. On the other hand, most members of the human race are only willing to invest a marginal effort for progress at the cost of indulgence since they aim for happiness instead of evolution. As a result, we satisfy ourselves with being at the front of the room and exploiting livestock for our welfare. While few pay attention to what the Red Queen said next, "if you want to get somewhere else, you must run at least twice as fast as that," we must ask what happened to those who did run twice as fast or those who simply ran too fast to care about the cheers of others. They stepped outside the front door and disappeared from the sight of the public who remained inside, much like the others who ran too slowly and slid out the back door. We must acknowledge that the greatest men who ever existed are not those we celebrate today but those who have remained unknown across the long course of history. Imagine someone who advocated animal rights when even slaves were traded as commodities or someone who studied the elemental building block of the world back in the Stone Age. The records of their thoughts were long weathered and annihilated before any successor could possibly recognize and appreciate their value. Human wisdom drives us forward, whereas the upper limit of human wisdom—the inability to comprehend theories outside the room—imprisons us.

It was on insomnia-plagued nights that I journeyed into *Rainstorm of Tomorrow: The Ever-Flowing Banquet of Philosophy* to record cogitations stranger than fiction: the culprits behind my stolen sleep; the raging beasts of thought who know no weariness until the relief of dawn; the rebellious, nocturnal souls shed of daytime attire as social elites. On these nights, I could not stop wondering what those prophets experienced outside the room where the mass resided. Maybe they broke into another room of greater elimination speed and fiercer competition. Embattled by endless challenges and triumphs, they may lose themselves in the heavy fog of nihilism. Nihility is a pack of opportunistic wolves lurking in the shadows, leaving restless hunters in ravenous hollows. To eat or be eaten, hunters set out on a journey that is at once futile, halfway, and paradoxical. They scaled a mountain and turned back halfway, not because the scenery on the summit lacked beauty, but because it is just as beautiful. They hailed the sea to find no answer. No answer is the answer. They sold flowers in a field of flowers and preached miseries to the miserable world. They exploited every possibility the world could offer but did not indulge in any of them. Until then, they were banners for an epiphany: how narrow the world is compared to the immense potential of what life could be. A pity that most men, for fear of a wolf attack, curl themselves up inside a tin box named purpose and significance.

Renyuan Dong

Part One
Truth

Renyuan Dong

1

Tree Growing into the Soil with Its Roots Buried in the Air

Core Question: Is the world of nature knowable?

    The tree represents an existence of obscurity, mystery, metaphor, and silence. While its canopy can stretch up to several thousand square meters, its roots can cover an area of up to ten million. Such shocking, asymmetrical data prompted a nascent passion within me to carefully reimagine tree roots. Where to find a tree floating tranquilly in a lake, with its wanton crown stretching above shimmering, fluid moonlight; and beneath the water's surface, as neither a reflection nor an attachment, grows another "tree," its composition of interweaving, soil-delving roots discarded for an indiscriminate splay into the water? What a spectacular dual-tree picture it would cast upon the lake! Yet, this image is by no means symmetric, since the submerged tree is much more flourishing than its peer above the water—the part we normally see and recognize as a "tree." Such a scenery would challenge our habitual perspective, as we human beings commonly rank the primacy of an object's features on the basis of their "size." By such a metric, would not the "roots" be defined as the "trunk," the principal component of a tree, while the "trunk" instead assumes the role of the "roots"? Is it possible that the "trunk," which always comes to our mind first whenever the concept of a "tree" is elicited, is just the tip of the iceberg exposed by an unfathomable creature? Is it plausible that the roots, surviving in the rotting mire and interwinding through the dense soil, would instead represent the prime sign of a "tree" and its future growth? "Impossible!" retort arrogant humans, "It is the so-called 'tip of the iceberg' that shelters us from the summer heat and heavy rain. And after all, the dual-tree cast up and down the lake is merely something of dreams. In reality, no tree floats like a castle in the air. They are all solidly rooted in the soil and stretch actively toward the sky."

Indeed, the tree can be rooted in the soil and grow toward the sky. To some extent, even the discussion concerning whether the tree is growing in the air or the soil seems meaningless as long as we are satisfied with the interpretations of the "human world:" a collection of human minds and consequent thoughts of the external material environment, a self-interpretation of nature (or the creator's world if you believe in a creator). Yet, the world of nature—and the phenomena within it—is not subject to human minds. Just as there is never a single snowflake falling in pursuit of symbolizing "purity," there is never a flock of wild geese flying by with the intention of evoking homesickness in skyward onlookers. "You not being a fish yourself… how can you possibly know in what consists the pleasure of fishes?" (Zhuangzi, 2001, p. 67). The only way to reveal the truth of a tree is to ask the tree itself. Yet. the tree stands still. Then, think of yourself as a tree! If we hold steadfast to our human existence, it is difficult to comprehend that the tree grows into the soil rather than into the air. It takes only a shallow swamp to trap human feet, to say nothing of covering an entire body in dense soil. However, each creature has a suitable environment and adequate pressure for its own survival; an excessive amount would lead to an unbearable weight of being while insufficient pressure would dissolve our sense of reality. For trees, we cannot rule out the possibility that the air is an unbearably frivolous and ethereal presence in their lives, just as humans would suffocate at high altitudes due to the thin air and the consequent lack of oxygen. On the contrary, only the density of the soil manages to ease their minds. As their roots stretch through the gaps in the earth, they will never know whether a pile of soft soil or a piece of hard rock awaits them ahead. Thus, the growth itself becomes an adventure. This is the weight that trees must bear in their lives, and the wonder that human beings would never understand.

Humans have always tried to seek out "Truth." Yet, in this pursuit, we are often waylaid by cognitive biases and distortions rooted in the inherent limitations of the sensory channels that humans rely on to explore the world. We see this world through "human eyes" rather than through the "creator's eyes," a predisposition shared by all our senses. They present a colorful, fragrant, lively world to us yet one that is far from encompassing the entire being of nature. While many colors are registered by human eyes, there are even more varieties that fall outside our visible spectrum and are thus imperceptible to us, not to mention that our sensory channels can only perceive light, acoustic, chemical, and physical stimuli. We lack specific sensory channels for detecting other potential sources of information, such as magnetic induction, which made the acknowledgement and study of such phenomena impossible for a long time (before science came to our aid).

Imagine the world from the eyes of a bat! Through darkness, everything is represented by the crisp sound of stones breaking a lake's surface, each producing a different note, reverberating before gradually fading, just like the ripples that spread out to the water's shores. And what about the world of an insect with compound eyes? It is composed of stacked, contiguous TV screens, each playing the same program slightly out of sequence. Thus, sensory limitations lead to cognitive biases and distortions, granting each being its own "self-righteous" world.

Science and technology have not only supplemented our sensory ability and exploratory approach to external physical and chemical phenomena by augmenting our native senses but also corrected the cognitive errors caused by subjective feelings and emotions. For example, the essential motion status of a being is motive rather than static, and the descent time of a free-falling object depends on its mass rather than its size. Therefore, the sensory limitations mentioned above should be regarded as the limitations that remain after science and technology have enhanced humans' sensory ability and exploratory approach. These remaining sensory limitations lead to cognitive biases.

Aside from the restrictions imposed by our senses, we are also imprisoned in a cage of *time and space*, hindering the study of space-time phenomena at significantly different magnitudes, such as those at the scales of the universe or the microscopic world. For example, consider the following highly controversial hypothesis: The universe is not a concept of infinite time and space but rather the inner cavity of a giant creature, its organs and soft tissue being the nebulas and stars of our telescopes. So what about us? We human beings are something akin to bacteria living in that creature. In that case, are we probiotics or parasites? Are natural disasters and environmental changes movements of a universe-generated immune response to human overcrowding and pollution? Moreover, what is taking place in vitro of the giant creature? Perhaps there is another, even larger organism in comparison with which our universe (the giant creature) may be as small as a parasitic bacterium. The structure of nature may thus circulate endlessly. The reason why human beings cannot equivocate a boundless cosmos with a bounded inner body and hence cannot associate their stalwart selves with dismissible microbes is that we lack eyes big enough to behold the universe in one glimpse—nor can we shrink our bodies as Sun Wukong (the Monkey King)[1] did to enter the body of Princess Iron Fan. Therefore, we cannot comprehend the world of bacteria inside the human body.

"To be means to be perceived (*esse est percipi*)" (Berkeley, 2003, p. 32). The reason that I, an ardent materialist, am quoting George Berkeley, a representative idealist, is that this phrase means much more than is at first apparent: To be means to be appreciable by human beings. The existence of an object does not depend on whether it is sensed, but on whether it can be detected by the human sensory ability and exploratory approach. Even the retort in a satirical comic picturing Berkeley walking toward a cliff with his eyes closed, muttering, "to be means to be perceived" (implying that the cliff is not perceived by Berkeley but exists regardless), is not enough to refute his theory. The object not perceived may exist in a state of being temporarily unperceived. If it is *ultimately appreciable*, then it exists; as Berkeley finally arrives at the edge of the cliff, or even falls from the cliff, he would become aware of the cliff's existence. The implicit semantics of Berkeley's quote are: Even if we have tried every means of detecting an "assumed" object, yet there is still no way that it can be perceived or sensed, we should not assume that such an object exists. Whether or not one agrees with this argument informs their association with one of the two schools of epistemology: cognosciblism or agnosticism.

There are two major points of contention between cognosciblism and agnosticism: First, for those objects that we can perceive, does our perception reflect the nature of objects in the objective world? Given my previous argument that human sensory limitations entail cognitive limitations, you may answer in the negative. As we have always lived in the "human world," we can never capture the nature of the "objective world." However, there may be an extent to which you would disagree with this point of view. If I say there are people with ordinary vision, hypochromatopsia, and achromatopsia in this world, this would further imply that the nature of the ob-

---

1   Sun Wukong and Princess Iron Fan are characters of *Journey to the West*, a Chinese novel attributed to Cheng'en Wu. This scene happens when Sun Wukong shrinks himself and wreaks havoc inside the body of Princess Iron Fan, making her surrender and agree to lend him the Iron Fan.

jective world may not be as colorful as our ordinary vision suggests. You may then agree that worlds colored to different degrees are likely neither closer to nor farther away from the nature of the objective world. But if I were to say the "human world" is merely a projection onto three dimensions of the "objective world," which is actually 16-dimensional in its nature, you may find that such a notion sounds quite ridiculous.

Second, for those objects we cannot perceive, could they possibly exist in the objective world while being unappreciable to human beings? Suppose there is such a Substance A that could neither be detected by human sensory channels nor interfere with the objects or phenomena that are appreciable to human beings. Therefore, Substance A forever remains outside the cognitive field of human beings. Do we have sufficient grounds to assume that such Substance A exists? Opponents usually state that this assumption can never be falsified, and therefore requires no research. It is like "the dragon in my garage" (Sagan, 2011, p. 169): an invisible, floating, untouchable, fire-breathing dragon that spews heatless flame that neither burns nor blows anything away. You cannot think of any way to test whether it is really there. In contrast, we could raise another example named the non-existing dragonfly in the world of an ant: "The world is 2-dimensional in the eyes of an ant. If you lift the ant from the ground, it disappears in the eyes of its companions" (Luo, 2017, n. p.). Since ants lack the concept of "height" (strictly speaking, ants can perceive only a very limited range of altitudes) and there is no direct-interest between ants and dragonflies, the latter fly outside the former's cognitive world. Yet, they do exist. Ultimately, this kind of analogy is merely an inductive argument. No matter how many examples we may raise concerning the inability of creatures living at lower dimensions to recognize the existence of creatures living at higher dimensions, such argumentation could only imply that there is a big possibility that a substance unappreciable to humans *might* exist in the objective world. In order to prove it, we might have to wait like the ants in the prior example. Only on the day when the dragonfly falls to the ground when its life has come to an end can we finally *confirm* the existence of such "dragonflies" for the first time.

In terms of the knowability of nature, the advocates of cognosciblism would prevent you from worrying unfoundedly. Pessimistic advocates of agnosticism would warn you not to bite off more than you can chew. "Whereof one cannot speak, thereof one must be silent" (Wittgenstein, 2014, p. 3). And I, as an optimistic advocate of agnosticism, would suggest you "stay hungry, stay foolish" (Brand, 1972, back cover). More important,

I raised the hypothesis that "the universe might be contained within a giant creature" not to convince you (at least, not in this chapter) but rather to remind you that imagination is always possible in the pursuit of better explanations in today's world—a world where scientific explanations are all-encompassing and (seemingly) persuasive, a world where the unknown wonders are vanishing rapidly together with room for further improvement. Imagination would bring forth myths; imagination would bring forth religions; imagination would bring forth the "seeming" enemies of science, and because of that, imagination would eventually bring forth the groundbreaking progress promised by science or whatever name that speaks for "Truth" (if science were to be regarded as witchcraft by then).

2
The World As a Fundamentally Material Being

Core Question: Is the reality of the world material or mental? Or both?

Let's return to the metaphor presented in the title of the previous section, "The tree growing into the soil with its roots buried in the air." A botanist would be confused by this phrase before discreetly telling you that the development of a seed into a tree is a process of the simultaneous growth of the roots and the trunk in opposite directions. When the seed is placed in fertile soil, the development of the roots will far outweigh that of the canopy, and the tree is more inclined to absorb nutrients from the soil to support its own nourishment. When the seed is placed in barren soil prevalent in urban greenery, however, the development of the roots may be restricted to a size similar to that of the canopy, and the tree will perform photosynthesis more actively through its canopy to make up for the lack of energy supplied from the soil. A botanist could even clarify all the biological and chemical reactions that take place, from the roots to the crowns and from the branches to the leaves. We regard this as a scientific concept and an objective expression.

As for ordinary people who do not have such complete knowledge of botanic growth, they would simply think that the tree is rooted in the soil and grows upwards into the air. This idea may not be as accurate as its scientific counterpart, but is still an efficient, concise expression in line with their daily experience. We regard this as an empirical concept and a common expression.

Earlier in the article, I mentioned "the tree growing into the soil with its roots buried in the air," arguing that the growth process itself ought to be described adversely. The tree is rooted in the air and grows downwards into the soil. The statement may be considered a rebellion and challenge to social norms. We regard this as a mysticism concept and a literary expression. As you can see, our concepts and expressions of the same object may vary. However, no matter what conceptual schemes or linguistic practices we are dealing with, they are all built and constructed within our minds, hence their being called mental phenomena.

For a curious materialist (or, in a broader sense, a realist) who dares to admit his/her own limited knowledge, the world would undergo a three-tiered decomposition from its own self to our cognitive experience. The first tier is the "thing-in-itself world (the objective world)," which is independent of the will of mankind.

The second tier is the *part* (if you believe there are entities unappreciable by humans while existing in the objective world) or the *dimension* (if you believe what we have perceived is merely the cognizable, 3-dimensional projection of the objective world, not the thing-in-itself world which is of higher dimensions) of the first-tier world that falls within the scope of human cognition. This tier is usually called the "objective world appreciable by humans" and becomes our empirical object. Even though science and technology are committed to dragging more parts of the objective world (the first tier) into our scope of experience (the second tier), such expansion has its own limit. The second tier would never completely overlap with the first tier and truly become the world-in-itself.

The third tier is the formation of different kinds of cognitions, interpretations, and conceptual schemes by mankind after experiencing the second-tier world and is commonly known as our "mental world." It is also the "human world" mentioned earlier; to be precise, it should be referred to as the "human-interpreted world" or the "human-digested world."

It is noteworthy that neither do these three-tier worlds refer to three completely different worlds, nor do they stand for the mind–body dualism in traditional eclecticism: the combination of the first and second tiers, referred to as the external material (objective) world, and the third tier, defined as the inner mental world, which is the subjective reflection of the external objective world, the existence of which relies on the former two. Instead, these three tiers indicate the same object, the fundamentally material world, by which I indicate that all mental phenomena and subjective concepts in the third-tier world are material in nature. *They are essentially matter.*

All kinds of thoughts, memories, and ideas are already material in nature by the time they are stored in our brains in the form of bioelectric currents flowing throughout the central nervous system. Even though we cannot pull a piece of memory out of our brains with a magic wand, like Dumbledore did in *Harry Potter*, there are still many ways to materialize these products of the mental world, such as by delivering lectures, publishing books, broadcasting via the Internet, or even creating civilized crafts based on one's own ideology, like architecture, spacecraft, experimental tools, and the like. (If we were to one day realize the idea of sharing via an inter-brain exchange of bioelectric currents, we might be able to save all these materialization efforts.)

These thoughts and theories, generated by and stored as bioelectric currents, are included in the material objects of the first-tier world. The fact that they are created and generated by humans makes them empirical objects of the second-tier world. They are further studied and interpreted by our posterity like any other objects from the second-tier world so as to be further improved upon and developed in the third-tier world. We should not forget ourselves as part of the objective world as well. Therefore, those "achievements of civilization" and "thought matter" generated by us will continuously enrich and supplement the contents of the objective world in which we live.

If we state that thoughts and concepts are "mental" in nature and thus distinguish them from the rest of the external objective world, the nature of which is "material," idealists could argue that humans experience their mental world firsthand and that the external objective world, which mind–body dualism claims to be a projection source for the mental world, may not exist at all. Just like the example at the beginning of this paragraph demonstrated our perceptions and expressions toward the "tree," which is no more than an ordinary object, varied extensively. Idealists would further argue, "There are no such external objects but arbitrary and casual mental phenomena. If these mental phenomena are the reflections of external objects, they would not lack universal unity." Therefore, we will try to settle the question at its root by proving that all mental phenomena are indeed matter, such that they are "arbitrary and casual" matter.

All mental phenomena are matter, rather than beings affiliated to matter or relying on the existence of matter. The nature of the human mind, as the aggregate of the plethora of mental activities, is a restless, boiling electric ocean. The mind at "peace" does not refer to a sense of tranquility caused by a gurgling stream of ions, but rather to the gurgling stream of ions itself. Likewise, the mind in "fury" does not refer to a sense of eruption caused by a downpouring waterfall of ions, but rather to the torrential waterfall of ions itself. The reason why the mind becomes matter while being so arbitrary and unruly is that the brains of different individuals have constructed different watercourses for streams of ions to flow through. Therefore, even with the same external projection source, some of the watercourses are wide and level, creating a flow of ions that resembles a gurgling river; while others are curved and steep, and its flow of ions turbulent—even developing into a pouring waterfall on occasion.

I will try my best to explain the mechanism of mental phenomena in a more scientific and objective way despite this being a philosophical work. Referencing the paragraph above, the watercourses are the neuronal structures whose contents are electric charges (a physical property) rather than ions (matter). When a neuron is at rest, it maintains an interior (cytoplasm) voltage of about -65 mV, which is much less than the +50 mV charge outside of the cell; this is achieved by proteins called Na^+/K^+-ATPases that pump 3 Na^+ into the cytoplasm for every 2 K^+ out, thus maintaining a net efflux of positive charge. Much like a ball poised on the crest of a hill or an apple drooping from a branch, this polarization (difference in voltage) across the cell's membrane contains inherent, potential energy; given the smallest motion, the ball would tumble down the hill, the apple would fall from the tree, and the electric current would flow across the membrane to reach the same voltage on both sides, the equilibrium potential. This store of energy is expended to send signals to other neurons: An influx of extracellular Na^+ (or other positive ions) into a neuron depolarizes a site on its membrane, increasing the relatively negative voltage inside the cell; if the voltage inside the cytoplasm rises above the threshold of -55mV, voltage-gated ion channels open and cause an explosive influx of Na^+. This sharp change in polarization (from -65 mV to +40 mV) prompts similar depolarization phenomena at adjacent sites on the membrane— what amounts to a chain reaction of depolarization is transmitted along the lengths of the neurons' projections (axons and dendrites). This event is called an action potential,[2] and a neuron in which this phenomenon occurs is said to "fire." When the action potential reaches a protrusion at the end of an axon, the depolarization triggers the release of chemical compounds (neurotransmitters) into a space that constitutes a confluence of different

---

2   For an animation demonstration of the action potential, please refer to the web video at https://en.wikipedia.org/wiki/Action_potential.

neurons (the general area of connections is known as a synapse, and the inter-neuron space as a synaptic cleft). The neurotransmitters are emitted from the membrane of the first neuron, cross the synaptic cleft, and bind to receptors on the membranes of surrounding neurons. Depending on the neurotransmitter and consequently the postsynaptic receptor, either one of two events will occur: depolarization or hyperpolarization (an excitatory or inhibitory postsynaptic potential, respectively). The latter resembles the initial depolarization of the membrane, except instead of an influx of positive ions, extracellular Cl^- (or other negative ions) is brought into the cell; the membrane is thus further polarized, and the generation of an action potential is inhibited. A given neuron features thousands of both events occurring simultaneously. The depolarization and hyperpolarization phenomena are transmitted from the dendrites (the projections that receive the neurotransmitters at the synapse) to the body of the neuron (the soma), where the changes to the intracellular voltage summate. If their net effect reaches the action-potential threshold, the signal will be propagated from the soma to the axon. The nerve impulse would thus continue to be transmitted. Of note, excitations do not vary in magnitude: once a membrane has depolarized to +40 mV, the sodium channels close. Voltage-gated ion channels emit K^+ from the cytoplasm, and the Na^+/K^+-ATPases carry on maintaining a relatively negative voltage inside the cell. As +40 mV is the only magnitude at which a neuron can be excited, the intensity of human emotion or the strength of human thought, represented by the strength of electrical signals, therefore does not depend on the voltage reached or quantity of neurotransmitters, but rather on the frequency at which a given neuron is excited or the number of neurons concurrently releasing the same neurotransmitter.

But how can a neuron account for complex mental activities and advanced thought processes? It is the complex network formed by millions of neurons and their trillions of connections. A single neon tube is ultimately monotonous, even if it can blink at different intervals; however, if we bundle up a large quantity of neon tubes together, they form an art installation of countless flickering images. The development of the human is a process by which connections among neurons are constantly refined for optimal performance. With experience, necessary connections are strengthened and those that diminish performance are weakened and ultimately lost. Sophisticated mental activities are thus achieved by a streamlined pathway of neuronal connections. As experiences differ from person to person, so do neural structures. Mental reactions to the same external stimulation thus vary across different people. Even in the same individual, neurobiological changes with age are concomitant with evolving mental responses to the same external stimulation. No wonder the idealists would find it hard to believe that the mind is such an "arbitrary and casual" matter.

Strictly speaking, mental activity, the transmission of electrical signals across a single neuron and between neurons, is the process of transmitting a positive voltage from the dendrite to the axon of a neuron and then onto the next neuron via the directional movement of Na^+ and other ions. In the case of a continuous conduction of electrical signals, if we connected the neurons of a pathway from head to tail into a straight line, we would be able to draw a wave bitmap. The membrane potential at the beginning of the line would rise sharply from a negative to a positive voltage before becoming negative again; this form would propagate seamlessly to the end of the line. Of course, the electrical signals within a single neural pathway are barely detectable. However, they accumulate in amplitude across a countless number of neural pathways, thereby supporting mental activity of sufficient intensity to manifest itself in consciousness. Such concurrent activity is detectable as what are commonly known as "brain waves." The directional movement of Na^+ refers to the movement of Na^+ entering and exiting an axon tunnel that features a rhythm and sequence, a bit like the "wave dance" performed by stadium audiences at a football match or a concert—perhaps an "ion wave dance" is a more apt description for the bioelectrical activity of the neuron. By means of such a one-way "ion wave dance," a positive voltage is delivered across one neuron—from its dendrite, to its soma, to its axon. Akin to waves of water, it is noteworthy that the Na^+ themselves do not flow along the axon tunnel. If we stir up waves in a sink and put a rubber duck on the water's surface, the waves would carry the duck away laterally, while the water molecules forming the wave would only move vertically. These Na^+ are just like the water molecules in the water wave. While the rubber duck displaced by the water waves is an exact object (matter), the positive voltage delivered by "ion waves" (the directional movement of Na^+) is merely a physical property or energy (electrical energy).

The definition of mental activities as "bioelectric currents" travelling along neural structures (In many cases, we tend to favor this definition as it is more direct and straightforward. Many 3D simulation charts demonstrating neural structures would also label a point of light representing the electrical signal flowing through the nervous system, as if it actually existed.) implies that mental activity is a form of energy in nature or a phenomenon caused by the motion of matter. I tend to define mental activities as Na^+ ions performing the "ion wave dance" together with other ions or molecules in neural structures, and thereby conceptually restituting mental activities to matter—to be precise, matter in a specific state of motion. Only when Na^+ ions move according to a certain rhythm and sequence can they be regarded as specific mental phenomena (the category of which is determined by the specific choreography of Na^+ motion). When Na^+ stands on the sidelines, we may only describe such a brain state as "a mind totally blank."

Besides rejecting "mental activities" as matter bereft of universal unity (across different individuals) and consistency (across time), many idealists further posit the existence of "innate ideas/priori knowledge" and refute the concept of an objective, externally sourced, permanent being. This contrasts with a quote by David Hume, the famous empiricist, from his *An Enquiry Concerning Human Understanding*: "All our ideas or more feeble perceptions are copies of our impressions [all our ideas are posteriori knowledge acquired from experience]" (2012, p. 10). So how should we explain the very existence of "innate ideas/priori knowledge"?

The so-called "a priori" is not heaven-sent but rather the inheritance of ancestral memory. Aptly put by the adage "like father, like son," this idea entails the convergence of a person's thoughts with those of their ancestors. Can specific ideas or concepts be inherited? The answer is yes. We know that genes are heritable. As genes control the expression of proteins that inform the physiology of the human body, the expression of proteins is also passed down from ancestors to their decedents. This further implies that the physiological structure of their bodies is identical, or at least similar. Such shared physiology may include nervous tissue in the brain. If specific ideas or concepts are analogous to the water flowing through a waterpipe, the structure of encephalic tissue is akin to the waterpipe itself. The directions and patterns of water flow through two different waterpipes are similar in response to the same external stimulus (e.g., the same water pressure or the same amount of water inflow) insofar as the structures of the waterpipes are similar. It would not be a surprise to find that a person holds ideas or beliefs similar to those of their parents or even grandparents.

The inheritance of ideas is often evinced by aesthetic ideals. If not being influenced by specific values, humans tend to regard curves as more beautiful than straight lines, a colorful palette more appealing than a monochrome one, music more mellifluous than noise, and a prosperous life more pleasant than a wanting one. The reason why humans favor curves over straight lines may be traced back to the memory of a uterus from one's infancy. Compared to rectilinear lines, curves may instill a softer, more protective feeling that continues to be preferred after infancy. The reason why humans favor colors over monochrome may be traced back to more ancient memories—when our ancestors still lived in a primitive, natural environment, where a colorful world represented daytime and the world cast in black-and-white meant that night had fallen. As diurnal creatures whose vision is limited in a monochrome world and whose audition is relatively weak, humans would have faced a higher risk from predators by night. Across generations, the mentality of looking forward to the colorful day and fearing the monochrome night would have become engrained in humans. The reason why humans favor music over noise simply reflects the fact that circumstances with rhythm or a relatively predictable course are preferable to unpredictable, chaotic alternatives; the former provides us with information we can use to act and therefore provides a greater sense of security than does the latter (Burke, 1966).

As you can see, many "innate ideas" of mankind across different races and cultures can be traced back to a distant memory of human ancestry, when humans regarded things *beneficial* to human survival as *true*, *virtuous*, and *attractive*, and those *harmful* as *false*, *evil*, and *hideous*. Such judgment itself is in line with the principle of utilitarianism: of pursuing collective interests and avoiding risks. Successive generations of idea inheritance, however, have retained the conclusions (what is true/virtuous/aesthetic and what is false/evil/hideous) and forgotten the reasons (because it's beneficial/harmful to human survival).

Today, the notion that "one gene controls the expression of one physiological feature" is outdated thanks to developments in the fields of genetics and epigenetics. Prevailing theories instead posit that one genotype[3] can yield multiple phenotypes,[4] and the expression of one physiological characteristic can depend on the synergy of multiple genes. Meanwhile, certain experiences or environmental changes can activate epigenetic

---

3 Genotype, also known as genetic type, is a general term for the entire genome of an organism.

4 Phenotype refers to the individual appearance, function, and other aspects of external manifestations.

modifications[5] to "temporarily" or even "semi-permanently" regulate the form of chromatin fibers, the material containing genes, and thus alter the expression of a specific gene and its consequent functions—just like adjusting the volume of a radio. To adapt to a novel environment, epigenetic modifications might temporarily turn off or reduce the expression of a specific gene—thereby decreasing the production of certain kinds of proteins (e.g. enzymes) and consequently, cells. If the "temporary" gene regulation benefits the organism in the long term, it can be retained and further consolidated as a "semi-permanent" regulation: the function of such a gene may remain shut down except under extreme conditions. In other cases, the "temporary" regulation can be easily reversed so that the gene can be re-expressed when the external environment has changed. Studies have shown that actions taken or adverse circumstances endured by one population have an effect on phenotypes of the following generation. For example, the generation following one that faced a food shortage is reportedly more vulnerable to obesity (Tobi et al., 2015). Epigenetic modifications could possibly account for such changes.

Genetic theory today equivocates the significance of the regulatory function of environmental factors on gene expression with that of the traditional role of genes themselves. The genotype is not like a computer program that, once compiled, will automatically run instructions without any interference from the outside world; it is more like an opera script, the performance of which could be adjusted according to the character of a theater or the preferences of an audience. Therefore, we need to amend our metaphor of "the encephalic waterpipe." If ancestors and descendants have the same genes for the expression of nervous tissue in the brain, then the structures of their encephalic waterpipes are likely to be the same. Yet, such waterpipes are not made of solid metal, but rather of a flexible, semiplastic, shape-memory alloy. Even if their initial structures are the same, the two waterpipes respond to different environments over time. Under the continuous scouring of different water inflows, the two waterpipes will be gradually bent into different arcs and shapes. Even so, the initial homogeneity makes one's brain structure or mindset still more similar to that of a relative than of a stranger. However, in cases of specific, urgent stimuli, especially those concerning life-and-death—say, if the waterpipe is heated up to an abnormal temperature or if the water pressure at the inlet

---

5   Epigenetic modification refers to the reversible regulation of gene expression through DNA methylation, histone modification, and non-coding RNAs, such as miRNAs. Such regulation does not cause changes in gene sequence but can be passed on to successive generations.

reaches a certain threshold—these flexible waterpipes will be restored to their original shape to ensure that the water inside is flowing according to the identical, time-tested pattern. Therefore, each individual would feature similar mental feedback and stress reactions to those of their relatives in response to threatening circumstances. It is acknowledged that, although the acquired experiences of each individual are different, we are surprisingly consistent with one another in some particular ideas and concepts—as if they are not derived from acquired experiences but rather belong to some kind of "priori knowledge" that one is born with. We now know that these common, innate ideas stem from the original shape of our encephalic waterpipes, manufactured from the same old mold.

3
All Questions Are Involved with Logos

*Core Question: What language should we use
to describe the material nature of the world?*

If we advocate that this world is fundamentally material—which is to say that all the objects described in our everyday language are essentially matter—we soon become embattled by difficulties of semantics. Some words refer to very "concrete" substances and engender no dispute, such as "apple." There are few who would confuse apples with pears. However, it is undeniable that many highly "abstract" and "conceptual" words are also used in our daily linguistic practices, such as "thought" and "virtue," along with those that are harder to define, such as the aforementioned "mind" or "mental activity." Moreover, there are other words that seem familiar and specific; yet, their material realities have always been questioned. Examples of this category would include "light," "time," "space," etc.

In trying to prove that every word indicates a being of matter, we may argue that the referents of those highly "abstract" and "conceptual" words do not exist in reality and that their creation actually reflects our abuse of the language. According to standard and proper linguistic practices, we should try our best to avoid using such words and even remove them from our vocabulary to avoid confusion and ambiguity. Let's look at an example:

> What is the "mind"? The mind is the communication process that neuron cells conduct through bioelectric currents.

Bioelectric currents run through the irregular pathways and structures of our nervous system to calculate, memorize and perform other functions just like the computer executes the program. Therefore, the "mind" is immaterial. Similarly, the wind is the flow of air. There is only "air" in the world. There is actually no such thing as "wind," but we are accustomed to taking the "wind" as matter as well (Running Mustang, 2010, n.p.).

The "wind" is not material in the author's opinion, so the word should not exist. Instead, we should rephrase the word "wind" as "the flowing state of air." "Breeze" should likewise be rephrased as "a gentle flow of air," and "hurricane" as "a violent flow of air," resulting in very lengthy terms and even longer sentences. Nevertheless, such rephrasing cannot accommodate all immaterial words. Here is one counterexample: the arrival of the young researcher gave the decadent academy a second "wind." It would be awkward to say, "the arrival of the young researcher gave the decadent academy a second 'flowing state of air.'"

Do you still remember the two definitions I gave for "mental activity" earlier?

(1) Bioelectric currents as a physical property of positive voltage conducted along neural pathways.

(2) Ions in directional movement along the neurons that generate and propagate the bioelectric currents.

The reason why I would prefer the second definition, even though it is not as intuitive as the first, is that it restitutes the "mind" or "mental activities" to the being of matter in a status of specific motion. I could therefore use the word "mind" to confidently refer to the groups of chemical ions performing complex movements within the nervous system, thereby simplifying my language. The author of the quote above adopts the first definition; he refers to "bioelectric current" as a more appropriate alternative to the immaterial definition of "mind." However, simply stating "bioelectric current" implies an intangible property that belies its foundation in the movement of chemical ions—essentially a phenomenon provoked by matter. If he truly advocated for the removal of abstract referents, every time he wanted to convey the meaning of "mind," "thought," or even "bioelectric current," he would instead write, "the directional movements of chemical ions across the neuronal membrane that is propagated along irregular pathways of connected neurons and structures of the nervous system," which is a pretty lengthy statement.

The practice of discarding and rephrasing is not uncommon in philosophical research. For example, many scholars think that concepts such as "time" and "space" do not actually exist in the objective world and are merely derivatives of the human imagination to help us better understand the world and its happenings. From their perspective, such words ought to be excluded from linguistics. (We will return to the concepts of "time" and "space" in the final chapter of this part.) However, substituting words corresponding to "mental" properties with those indicating "material" properties diminishes the conciseness and efficiency of language expression. Therefore, before making such a replacement, we need to determine whether such words can even be redefined as "material" properties—in other words, we would have to prove that every word in linguistics refers to a being of matter. I would first like to validate the following point of view: All "happenings," including "actions" (where the subject is usually human) and "phenomena" (where the subject is usually a natural object), are material as long as the subjects triggering the happenings are material entities. As for the first definition of "mental activity," the positive voltage conducted along neural pathways, it is not under proof; the agent of such an action or phenomenon is a physical property or energy instead of matter.

We usually define a "happening" as "the specific serial movement conducted by a material subject." We state "the specific serial movement" first only to emphasize that, no matter whoever or whatever the specific subject is (as long as it is material), a "happening" occurs as the result of a specific choreography completed by the subject. We tend to break down the whole serial movement into several steps to facilitate understanding: the start, the development, the end, and the aftermath. When educating our children, we stress the importance of recognizing these steps so that they can distinguish when a happening begins from when it ends. The subject may continue to move or act after one happening ends, but whatever they do does not concern the previously completed happening; rather, the subject is participating in another irrelevant "happening." Children without prepossessions, however, will assign extravagantly trivial steps to the entirety of the unknown serial movement; so trivial, that it finally reaches a point where a static subject assumes a specific posture for each unit of time—just like how we make animations by continuously flipping through pages of static pictures. For the children, the "happening" is "the material subject carrying out a series of postures in chronologic order"—that is, "the material subject completing a specific serial movement." We would not judge their cognition to be wrong in the objective sense, but rather recognize that the parts they emphasize (the material subject) are different from those on which we place emphasis (the serial movement). By "emphasis" we are referring to something subjective that has nothing to do with facts. Therefore, in the objective cognition of a "happening," the definition as "the specific serial movement conducted by a material subject" is equivalent to the definition, "the material subject (unspecified but recognized to be matter) completing a specific serial movement." "The wind is the flow of air" is equivalent to "the wind is the air that flows." The air remains air despite any displacement during its flow, thus maintaining its "material property" during the whole serial movement. The wind, as the air of motional status, is a being of matter as well. Therefore, the word "wind," due to its material property, has its own right to exist.

Based on this validation, we could further prove that all the vocabulary derived from detailed "actions" or "phenomena" are material—even the words that seem highly "abstract" and "conceptual." Let us consider the word "virtue" as an example. What would come to mind if you were asked to enumerate specific virtues? In China, language teachers humorously summed up cliché cases common in students' essays: return a wallet to its owner, offer one's seat to an elder, buy food for a beggar, help the blind avoid a barrier, do the chores for your mother, honor agreements to the letter, etc. (The subject of this rhyme is hidden since they do not need to be specified—in most cases, the heroes are the students themselves.) So how does the word "virtue" actually come into being? Let's suppose that a language teacher is correcting his students' journals. After he finished the first 10, he found that all of them had bragged about returning wallets casually found on the street to their respective owners as an exemplar of goodness. He then complained to other colleagues in the office, "These students' mindsets are far too narrow. Besides the theme of returning a wallet to its owner, isn't there anything else they could think of? Such as sharing their class notes with one another?" It was not long before he realized that he had complained too early. The next 10 journals lauded feats of yielding bus seats to elders, and the following five featured students helping their busy mothers with chores. Venting to his colleagues afterward, he repaired to a phrasing that would save him the time and trouble of reiterating the themes with which both he and his colleagues had already been too-well acquainted, "These students' mindsets are far too narrow. Besides entries singing praises of 'virtue,' isn't there anything else they could think of? Such as sharing their class notes with one another?" As you can see, "virtue" is introduced to summarize actions with the same common property and characteristic. It is noteworthy that 'virtue' does not refer to the common property or characteristic that these actions share, but rather to the actions themselves, which rank far more than three. In fact, "virtue" refers to all the countless actions that feature the common property and characteristic of being praiseworthy. Since "virtue" can be restituted to a collection of different actions of identical material property, it is material in essence as well.

However, say that one of the teacher's colleagues was not familiar with the word "virtue" and asked what it meant. If the teacher answered, "Virtue refers to the action/behavior reflecting superb moral standards," he gave a definition of "virtue" as an equivalent (the necessary and sufficient condition) to the word "virtue." Each detailed action cited in the rhyme above serves as a component and necessary condition of "virtue"; yet, "virtue" entails much more than the circumscribed list of actions. It is because of the very fact that the components of "virtue" cannot be exhausted that we would like to define it once and for all. If we study the word "virtue" from its definition, we encounter words of ambiguous semantics, such as "superb," "moral," and "standard," which in turn induce us to regard "virtue" as a spiritual concept of an abstract composition, as if it were an innate idea bestowed by a god upon his favored mankind. As a consequence, we as human beings would be captured in an illusory theory of good-nature. But as long as we find specific actions constituting "virtue" in our daily life, we will find the fundamentals of its material property in the objective world.

Let us further analyze a type of more advanced words, the so-called "concepts" of the "triangle," "temperature," and so forth. It is generally believed that a "concept" is the cognitive result that humans extracted from certain material entities. "Concept" cannot exist independently in nature; it must dwell in material entities and manifest itself only through human cognition. These conditions engender two doubts: First, do "concepts" actually exist in the objective world? Are they real entities? In fact, even if we pick up a triangular-shaped piece of stone, we don't see a "triangle," but a "stone." Only when we have summarized the common shape of a large number of triangular stones can we possibly conceive of the concept of a "triangle." However, the concept of a "triangle" can manifest itself in the objective world under certain circumstances. Imagine that we are the cave men from Plato's famous metaphor who have been captured in a cave with our limbs bound. The only way for us to recognize our world is to look at the images that appear on the rock wall in front of us. Should a triangular-shaped stone be illuminated by a torch behind us, all we would see projected on the rock wall is a "triangle." For the cave men, the "triangle" is a real, tangible entity. (Ironically, they do not spare much thought for the possibility of the "stone"—the projection source.) The existence of "temperature" can be proved likewise. Snakes have thermoreceptors between their noses and eyes, enabling them to "observe" colors of different warmth on the infrared spectrum; the relative temperatures arrayed across external objects thus enable them to distinguish their prey. For snakes, "temperature" is a tangible entity. It is noteworthy that the validation of one concept's existence does not guarantee its accurate and essential description as a property in a material entity. For example, suppose the objective world is composed of 16 dimensions. Therefore, the "essential shape," as a property of the stone from our example, should accordingly be 16-dimensional (a word not invented yet). The "triangle" is such an entity that is no more than a "projected shape" of the "essential shape" on a 2-dimensional surface. However, this also applies to objects that can be directly perceived by our sensory channels. Concepts, together with other directly appreciable objects, are both real entities; yet, neither of them guarantees an accurate description of the "essence" of the material world. But for reasons unknown and surely unsound, humans tend to rely on their intuition and suspect their indirect cognitions. This results in their continuous questioning of the concepts that they had developed; yet, they take "seeing is believing" for granted.

The second doubt would be: Even though the "concept" exists, is it matter? In other words, are all existing entities matter? Here we can roughly define "matter" as a being made up of physical particles in the traditional sense. In considering this topic, we may encounter one biased and invalid argument: All concepts indicate certain properties of material entities. The "triangle" refers to an object's property of shape, whereas a certain "temperature" refers to an object's property of internal energy. Which is to say, since matter is a being containing various physical and chemical properties, and if these properties cannot exist independent of matter, then these properties are naturally matter as well; since the whole object under consideration is matter, its components are matter as well. We call such a method of argumentation circular reasoning. Those "concepts," referring to properties, are proved to be matter simply because we defined those physical and chemical properties in advance as the components of the matter. "On what grounds can we arrogantly decide that these physical and chemical properties—also called different types of energy nowadays—are affiliated with the existence of matter, and are therefore components of matter," so refute idealists, "and not the opposite?" Idealists in the 21st century do not deny the existence of "matter," instead they advocate the objective reality of "mind/spirit" as well—the latter features a fashionable new name of "energy" under the package of technology nowadays. Idealists further argue: "Matter might exist, but energy is now considered to be the core essence of the objective world. Energy is so fragile and elusive that it must reside in matter to preserve its existence, as a hermit crab must inhabit a solid shell. If we were to visit a hermit crab, we would first encounter its external shell. By 'knocking on the door,' we would engage with the soul living within the shell. Thus, we cannot mistake the shell itself for the shy host who hides inside. Likewise, the energy dwelling in the material shell is the soul of this world and embodies its essential laws."

As this approach does not yield a satisfactory validation of the material reality of concept, we must seek other proofs. We must admit that we are neither cave men nor snakes, and are thus unable to tangibly detect concepts. Concepts are mental phenomena resulting from all kinds of human mental activities. Thus, they can ultimately be viewed as micro-physiological architecture and defined by biological language. Once again, there are two definitions for "mental activity" based on (1) bioelectric currents—a wave of positive voltage conducted along the neural pathways—and (2) chemical ions (such as Na^+) in directional movement along the neurons that generate and propagate the biological currents. The reader might perceive both definitions as equally scientific and correct; though this may be true, these two definitions indicate notably different natures. The former treats the essence of mental phenomena, including concept formation, as energy, the microstructure of which is a wave. We may call this an "energy wave" (as opposed to the "matter wave" proposed by Louis de Broglie). On the other hand, the latter definition treats the substance of mental phenomena as matter. To prove that everything is matter, the best approach is to prove that the "energy wave" of the first definition is also matter. Then, regardless of the definition one holds to, mental phenomena are always matter-based entities.

The energy wave concept, which was used to indicate the transmission of energy in wave form as dependent on the material medium, has already become obsolete. Light, or any electromagnetic wave in the broader sense, was once regarded as energy. (Visible light is merely one group of electromagnetic waves within the visible spectrum. The electromagnetic wave family also includes invisible ultraviolet and infrared rays, etc.) However, light wave transmission does not seem to require any material medium, as it can occur in a vacuum. Could light possibly be a substance capable of radiating itself? In 1905, Einstein published a paper exploring the nature of light from the perspective of material particles, and introduced the light quantum concept (i.e., the "photon" of today). As the wave theory of light was dominant at the time, Einstein regarded his approach as merely "heuristic" (p. 132). While numerous experiments have confirmed the wave properties of light, consideration of light as composed of photons, i.e., discontinuous material particles, seems to successfully explain some of the phenomena that are inexplicable according to the wave theory of light. Thus, light seems to possess two natures. To explain some phenomena, we must view light as a continuous wave; however, we must regard it as being composed of material particles to explain other phenomena. This is the prototype of the wave-particle duality of light. In the century since Einstein's proposal, physicists have observed light waves in experiments designed to prove the wave property of light but have always found photons in those structures to prove the particle property of light. Experiments using apex instruments, such as interferometers, have revealed that light is neither a wave nor a particle, but rather an ambiguous mixture of these two properties. Hence, Niels Bohr remarked that physical reality depends on the observer's whim: "Look for a particle and you'll see a particle. Look for a wave and that's what you'll see" (Ananthaswamy, 2013, p. 37).

In 1924, Louis de Broglie proposed the "matter wave" concept, believing that all material particles (matter) possess the same wave-particle duality as light. According to this hypothesis, electrons also exhibit fluctuations, such as interference and diffraction, as evidenced by later experiments on electron diffraction. Since then, waves have no longer been regarded as energy only. A wave may represent energy, but may also represent matter. The two definitions are not clearly bounded without intersection.

With the gradual development of quantum mechanics, the electron cloud model replaced Rutherford's planetary model describing atomic structure. The electrons in the electron cloud model perform high-speed motions within a spherical space around a nucleus, without fixed orbits or patterns. Every point illustrated in the electron cloud represents the probability of one electron being present at that location, rather than the exact location of that electron. Some radical modern quantum physicists claim that observation of the internal structure of an atom under an electron microscope reveals a tornado-like energy vortex composed of high-speed quarks and photons. They also state that, at further magnification, all that remains is a physical void. Elementary particle theory holds that quarks and photons differ according to their self-spin characteristics. Quarks are categorized as "fermions" and can be understood as "matter particles," while photons are categorized as "bosons," media facilitating interactions between substances that correspond to energy instead of matter. Recent experiments, however, have shown that compression of energy to high density, which makes bosons collide with each other at extremely high speeds, generates matter (fermions, such as electrons). However, the entire process is extremely inefficient and the generated symbiotic pair of particles (electrons and their antimatter particles, i.e., positrons) is quickly annihilated (Yu et al., 2019).

In summary, we can conclude that "matter" is the condensation of high-density "energy" on the macroscopic scale at low-velocity space-time, whereas "energy" is the release of "matter" on the microscopic scale at high-velocity space-time. The two (matter and energy) are essentially one. Our argument appears to have overshot its original goal of proving that mental phenomena (represented by bioelectric currents or brain waves) correspond to matter, as evinced by wave-particle duality. However, wave-particle duality, together with other theories of quantum mechanics, has gone too far and almost proven equivalence between energy and matter. Therefore, we can regard mental phenomena as matter, just like the neural pathways from whence they are generated. Alternatively, we can regard neural pathways (and any other physiological architectures in our bodies) as energy, identical to the mental phenomena and activities that they produce. Under the condition that matter is energy and vice versa, it is pointless to become trapped in idealism or materialism when describing the world. This predicament is identical to that encountered when one is asked to prove that all phenomena in nature are determined by causal relationships. By trying too hard, one ultimately denies free will.

The development of quantum mechanics has uncovered the unification of matter and energy at the microscopic level, forcing re-examination of their definitions and the boundaries between them. Under the framework of Newtonian classical mechanics, through which understanding of matter gradually matured, an object is regarded as matter because it can be cognized by humans as a definite mass occupying a specific extension in space-time. However, according to Einstein's theories of relativity, mass and extension are neither fixed nor objective properties, but can change consistently according to the object's motion state. The mass and extension of a given object observed at any given time can simply be a sensory illusion. Take the extension (length) as an example. According to the theory of relativity, higher object velocity corresponds to smaller extension (length) from the perspective of a stationary observer. This concept is reflected by a famous Chinese idiom: "a glimpse of a white horse flashing past a chink in a wall,"[6] which describes the phenomenon in which the body of a galloping horse seems to be reduced in length so that it can flash by a chink in the blink of an eye. If the white horse instead galloped on a three-dimensional (3D) spiral path at an extremely high speed (close to light speed), it would not only appear to be shorter in length to a stationary observer, but all its dimensions would seem to be reduced to zero, as if its extension (volume) no longer existed. If we define matter as something occupying a definite extension in space-time, could the white horse still be regarded as a material entity in this motion state? One might argue that the reduced body of the galloping horse is merely a visual illusion of the observer due to their different motion states. If the observer ran as fast as the white horse (or rode the horse itself) so as to be stationary relative to its motion, the observer could still measure the actual body size of the horse. The length/volume measured by an observer who is stationary relative to the target is called the "proper" length/volume of the target. However, the question remains as to whether an observer can remain stationary relative to the observation target at all times, so as to always obtain proper measurement results. It is quite difficult, if not impossible, to achieve such conditions in the microscopic world; for example, when attempting to measure the size of an electron orbiting a nucleus at extremely high speed. First, it is difficult to determine the extended boundary of an electron in the microscopic world (as the electron is also composed of other elementary particles, such as photons and quarks, with space intervals). Second, it is difficult to mimic its high-speed movement to maintain a stationary perspective relative to the electron.

Given these restrictions, we must compromise on the measurement method, by measuring the radius of an electron in motion first and then re-calculating its proper radius at rest, based on formulas from the theory of relativity (parameters such as electron position and velocity are also required for this calculation). However, the Heisenberg Uncertainty Princi-

---

6   This is a metaphor by Zhuangzi originally referring to the quick passage of time, like a white horse flashing past a chink in a wall. The time required for a galloping horse to pass through a chink seems shorter from the perspective of a stationary observer than from the moving horse itself. As length = speed × time, the length of the horse's body estimated by a stationary observer is much shorter than its actual length.

ple states that the position and momentum (velocity) of the same electron cannot be precisely measured at the same time. (Therefore, the proper radius and consequently the extension of the electron at rest cannot be determined precisely.) With that in mind, the following question arises: Can we always regard the electron as matter if its extension appears and disappears at different positions and irregular velocities?

We now proceed to a discussion of mass after extension. The energy of any substance can be defined as the sum of the rest energy contained in its mass and its kinetic energy:

$$E = mc^2 + \tfrac{1}{2}(mv^2) = mc^2 + K \qquad (3.1)$$

Where mc^2 is the rest energy contained in the mass m, $K = \tfrac{1}{2}(mv^2)$ is the kinetic energy, v is velocity, and c is the speed of light. When the object is stationary, K is zero and the object possesses only mc^2. Therefore, in the case of self-energy conservation (without an external energy supply), whenever a stationary object begins to move, it must consume some part of its m in exchange for v, by converting some of the mc^2 to K. This is also the mechanism that yields weight loss through running. However, the mass consumed during running $\Delta m = \tfrac{1}{2}(mv^2)/c^2$, where $v^2/c^2 \to 0$, is almost negligible, as the running speed v is significantly smaller than c. (This is unfortunate from a weight loss perspective.) In contrast, whenever some m is consumed (regardless of the size of Δm), the generated kinetic energy ΔK converted from the lost rest energy $\Delta E = \Delta mc^2$ is significant, because c is larger. Therefore, some of the plots presented in comics are not merely fantasies without basis, but rather well-informed explorations.

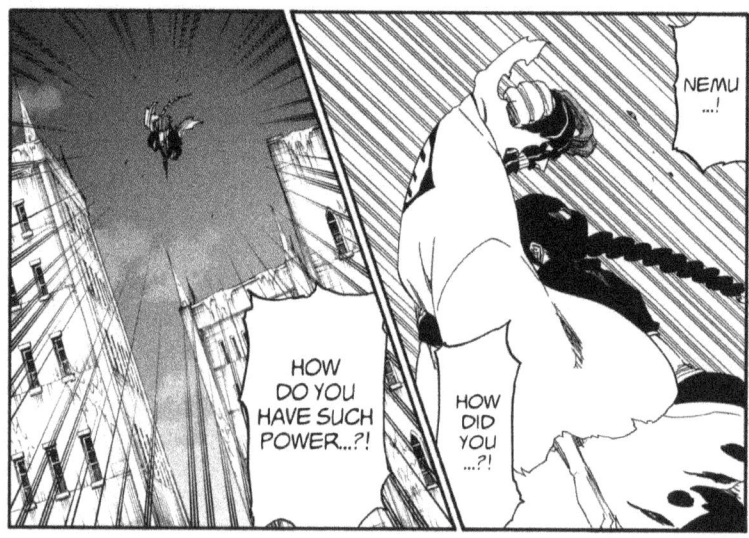

Figure 3.1. Excerpt from *Bleach*. Source: Kubo (2015).

Fig. 3.1 is an excerpt from the Japanese manga *Bleach*. The heroine has just sacrificed 0.8% of her body tissue in exchange for unparalleled kinetic energy and destructive power, allowing her to defeat her enemy (the giant hand in the top column) with just one strike.

We can deduce Einstein's famous mass-energy equation from the energy equation given in (3.1); the derivation process is omitted here:

$$E = mc^2 = \gamma m_v c^2 \qquad \gamma = \frac{1}{\sqrt{1-\left(\frac{v}{c}\right)^2}} \qquad (3.2)$$

Here, γm_v represents the relative mass of the object in a specific motion state. Note that the γm_v of an object increases with its kinematic velocity during acceleration. To achieve this acceleration, the object must be supplied with external energy, inducing an increase in its total energy. Without this supply, the object can only maintain its previous motion state; i.e., it remains at rest or exhibits continuous uniform motion due to self-energy conservation. Photons have no relative mass at rest. However, they adopt a velocity slightly smaller than c when traveling through air or other media, thereby obtaining a relative mass when in motion (this explains the existence of light pressure). If matter is defined as something occupying a definite mass in space-time, can photons, and other bosons (media facilitating interactions between substances), also be regarded as matter?

The traditional definition of matter as an entity occupying a definite mass and extension in space-time fits well with explanations of macroscopic phenomena but appears limited when applied to the microscopic world and high-speed phenomena. Scientists working in the field of quantum mechanics have attempted to reconcile and unify the concepts of matter and energy from the traditional adversarial relationship by introducing the concept of wave-particle duality and extending its application scope indefinitely. Instead of a simple conclusion that matter is equivalent to energy and vice versa, energy seems to be slightly dominant in this ontological debate. This is because energy is ubiquitous, whereas the formation of matter is fortuitous on the scale of the universe. At the macroscopic level, any substance/matter can be interpreted as energy condensation; however, physically formless energy-transfer phenomena are nevertheless ubiquitous. At the microscopic level, almost any particle pertaining to matter or phenomena can be restored to energy. "In the late 19th century, a perspective gained traction in which the traditional emphasis on physical matter (i.e., tangible matter such as earth or water, or microscopic building blocks such as atoms) was rejected. Instead, ultimate reality was said to be based on power, forces, and energy states, which somehow produce matter as effects. A still more modern concept is the view that reality consists of neither matter nor energy, but some more basic element that can manifest as either matter or energy" (Solomon, 1982/2008, p. 141). Through the ongoing study of quantum mechanics, this perspective has been revived in the 21st century.

Similar to materialism (or realism), idealism has a long development history. The initial subjective idealism declared that "I as subject am God," with everything else being mental phenomena generated by me. This school of thought could be the belief of one person but never of a group of people. That is, if two or more individuals held the same belief, they would be in conflict over "who on Earth is God." To overcome this problem, objective idealism was later founded to declare that everyone lives in one spiritual world created by God, who is an objectively real entity non-identical to one's subjectivity, and upon whom one's subjectivity is dependent and prone to manipulation. Thus, the essence of one's ego and the essences of the empirical objects one perceives are included in the collection of spiritual creations. This school of thought gradually evolved in conjunction with religious decline and scientific progress, surviving in the modern atheist-dominant age by replacing the concept of "God" with "Nature" and rephrasing "the discipline of the creator's world" as "the natural law." At present, the relationship between body and mind (matter and energy) is like that between the head and tail of the same coin: different sides of the same entity. Therefore, the reader should agree that regardless of the linguistic system (either that of materialism or of idealism) adopted to describe the world, the selected language should state facts common to the other language, as matter and energy have been incorporated into one concept.

However, the worldview overthrow induced by the advent of quantum mechanics has been even more far-reaching. Heisenberg's Uncertainty Principle and Bohr's Complementarity Principle (as an explanation of the former) have brought some of the common ideas advocated by idealists, which are not well-accepted by materialists, back to the stage again. This implies that the endless debate over materialism and idealism is not based on the *ontological question alone* (the world as a matter being vs. the world as a mental creation), but also on the *systematic perspectives* of the world that will be derived from the core setting, once the ontological question is answered with matter or soul. Such derivatives would include but not be limited to the following: Is the world knowable (cognosciblism vs. agnosticism)? Are there any objective laws or disciplines describing the world's operation (causal relationship vs. probability theory)? How should we function in this world (scientific research for the sake of absolute truth vs. scientific research for the sake of maximum utility)? As a result, Einstein is also among those scholars who had (or still have) reservations about quantum theory, although he introduced the concept of "light quanta" and, in a sense, set the scene for quantum research.

4

Quantum Theory and the Ultimate Aim of Science

Core Question: Is the purpose of science purely to seek truth or to guide practice?

The Heisenberg Uncertainty Principle states that the position and momentum of a given particle cannot be accurately measured at the same time. In the trade-off of quantum interactions, the more precisely the position of a given particle is determined, the less precisely its momentum can be known, and vice versa. This uncertainty reflects the limitations of our research methods when applied to the microscopic world. A special microscope would be required to observe electron movement. An ordinary microscope uses visible light to illuminate an object and then concentrates the reflected light to form an image. However, the visible-light wavelength is much longer than the wavelength of electron motion; therefore, it cannot be used for accurate measurement of electron positions. To observe electrons, in theory, we would need a microscope to emit light with a very short wavelength at a very high frequency, such as gamma rays. However, the energy of gamma-ray photons is extremely high. When a photon of such light strikes an electron, it inevitably affects the speed of the electron itself, thereby interfering with precise measurement of its kinetic energy. To reduce interference with the electron speed, low-energy photons must be used for electron detection; that is, light with a longer wavelength and lower frequency is employed. However, use of long-wave light means that the electrons cannot be positioned accurately. In other words, we cannot have our cake and eat it too.

In the macroscopic world, we can clearly distinguish between the behavior of the observation itself and that of the observed object; there is no interference between the two. In quantum physics, however, we cannot avoid the observer effect; that is, measurements of certain systems cannot be performed without affecting those systems. As a result, Heisenberg stated: "It is meaningless to speculate the nature of the object which cannot be observed and measured." Further, as an approximate description of the observation only can be attained, "there are only probabilistic events, but no ground for causality and determinism in quantum physics" (Kumar, 2012, p. 200).

Bohr established the Complementarity Principle to further explain that the Uncertainty Principle is inherent in the properties of all wave-like systems, as electrons also demonstrate wave-particle duality. While the particle property of the electron suggests that it possesses a clear position and velocity at any given time, its wave property obscures manifestation of these properties. We can develop a complete understanding of our research object only by combining information on both its particle and wave aspects. Bohr also agreed that it is meaningless to assume that there is a "real objective world" behind the "perceived statistical world." The purpose of science is not to determine "what nature is," but to "expand our range of experience and summarize those experiences in order" (Kumar, 2012, p. 210).

The two masters of quantum theory, Bohr and Heisenberg, thus presented some unpleasant views from a philosophical perspective, including the famous "to be means to be perceived (*esse est percipi*)" of George Berkeley. Those scientists may not have argued about whether an objective world exists independent of human perception. However, they would have both agreed that such an assumption of an unappreciable world is meaningless; on the contrary, researching the perceivable world is the priority of scientific practice.

Further, through their perception-based results, which indicate uncertainty, Bohr and Heisenberg affirmed that the quantum world is composed of accidental and probabilistic events, which in turn negates the existence of causality and determinism. Is this uncertainty actually the correct perception of the quantum world? It may be; however, Heisenberg's explanation is insufficient. The Uncertainty Principle only indicates that we currently lack effective methods to conduct objective research on the microscopic level without interfering with the research object. If, in theory, such a "best of both worlds" microscope can never be invented, other methods of observing electron motion should probably be developed. For example, "atom cloning" could be considered. If we could clone another atom identical to the atom being observed (including the electron movement at any given time), we could then use a gamma-ray-emitting microscope to precisely locate the position of a given electron in one of the atoms, while using another microscope to emit long-wavelength light to precisely measure the velocity (momentum) of the same electron in the cloned atom. Hence, accurate data on both attributes could be achieved simultaneously. Other approaches would include reducing the observer's size to microscopic level or expanding the object's size to macroscopic level so as to remove the extremely large dimensional differences between the observer and object. Such a mechanism could potentially be achieved in the future under the guidance of relativity theory. That is, if Observer A were to travel toward Atom B (the observation target) at a speed close to that of electrons, Observer A would appear to shrink in size and eventually disappear from the perspective of other researchers at rest (because of the length contraction effect caused by acceleration). However, the fast-travelling Observer A himself would not notice any changes in his own body size. Rather, as he would eventually reach the electrons orbiting the nucleus and remain stationary relative to those objects, the microscopic structure of Atom B would expand before his eyes and become perceivable. Alternatively, if we could gradually attenuate the gravitational pull of the nucleus without destroying the stable structure of Atom B, the originally contracted atom would expand in volume to the macroscopic level, and the electron velocity would decelerate to a level that could be recorded by laboratory apparatus. (According to the equivalence principle, weakening a gravitational field induces the same phenomena as deceleration).

Through the various thought experiments mentioned above, we can eventually determine that (I) electrons rotate around the nucleus in an elliptical orbit similar to that of a planet; or (II) they jump from one orbit to another in a random manner; or (III) they collide with each other like snooker balls and then disperse through a spherical space around the nucleus. Only when we have successfully observed electron trajectories without interfering with the electrons themselves can we claim that we have conducted sufficient study of the quantum world. For as long as we are unable to observe electron trajectories, we must acknowledge our temporary limitations, instead of negating the existence of objective reality. With sufficient scientific study, electron position and momentum could be measured accurately and simultaneously. However, some new challenges might emerge. Let us suppose that the electron groups of different atoms of the same element were observed to perform different movement patterns, i.e., I, II, or III, or a mixture of these three modes. Thus, although these atoms would be categorized as one element because of common properties, such as their atomic structures, their electron movements would present unique characteristics and distinct behavioral patterns—like different individuals of the same species—making it impossible for us to identify any regular order from their performance. In that case, we would encounter another uncertainty (or unpredictability, to be precise). That is, although we could accurately measure the behavior of a given individual, we could not summarize the commonality of the group and predict its future development.

In fact, an increasing number of studies have revealed that many microscopic structures previously assumed to be determined by physical mechanisms have exhibited "free will" or human-like "social behaviors." For example, researchers at Basel University have reported that the neurons in human brains are linked together like a social network (Cossell et al., 2015). Although each neuron is connected to many others, only a few neurons that are very similar to each other establish the strongest connections, just as we tend to develop intimate relationships with those who share our interests or values. We may then ask whether the "free will" or "accidental behaviors" exhibited by microscopic particles refute causality and determinism. Let us take the stock market as an example. The closing price of any stock on the market is determined by the overall trading behaviors of each stockholder, which may be influenced by many factors; e.g., their future perception of the stock market, their previous investment experience, their character, and even their dreams of the previous night. Advocates of strong determinism argue that they can exhaust all factors that form the cause of every trading behavior, but opponents of this theory believe that these influencing factors only limit the range of possible behaviors, with the final trading behavior essentially being determined by the stockholder's free will (note that advocates of strong determinism regard free will as merely an expedient when all causative factors cannot be exhausted).

To advance this argument without detriment, it can be supposed that each stockholder's trading behavior stems from their own free will. We should also acknowledge that, regardless of the thoroughness with which past market trading charts are analyzed, only a highly probable but approximate estimate of the stock market's future trend can be established at best. We must then ask whether the "contingency" of each individual's trading behavior further contributes to the "chaos" of the stock market's outcome. The answer is "no." Rather, these "contingent" trading behaviors determine the final "contingent" stock market outcome. No matter how "contingent" the value fluctuations of the independent variables and the dependent variable are, this situation is ruled by the causal relationship—provided that the mathematical equation describing the relationship between the two variable types is unchanged. From this perspective, causality is an objective reality independent of the "contingent" or "regular" manifestation of the microscopic individual's behavior. (In fact, it is the very "contingent" manifestation of both the independent variables and the dependent variable that conceals the causal relationship between the two.) In the stock market, the closing price of any stock is determined by the relationship between supply and demand on that day. If the stock purchase demand exceeds the supply, the stock price rises, and vice versa. This is the eternal principle of any market operation, as the relationship between supply and demand determines the market price.

Whether different occurrences obey a causal relationship is one thing; whether we can apply these causal relationships to accurately predict the future is entirely another. Even if there is a causal relationship between different occurrences, it is difficult for determinism to guide practice for two reasons. First, the collection of information on all independent variables is difficult in reality. For example, in the stock market, all the trading behaviors of each investor can barely be tracked. Second, changes in the independent variables and the dependent variable often occur simultaneously, and there is no time gap in which predictions can be made (or in which prospective values can be attached to predictions). For example, even if all the investor trading behaviors concerning one specific stock were recorded, when could we predict the closing price of this stock with the best accuracy? Say we decide that it is when the last investor makes his/her final decision before the close of day. However, the closing price of the stock is simultaneously determined as soon as that last investor makes this decision, which in turn renders our prediction meaningless. This is not to say that determinism has no utility. It still plays a major role in experimental design and theoretical modeling where we can specify the value of independent variables at will and make predictions before the final result is revealed.

Finally, both Heisenberg and Bohr believed that objective reality without observation does not exist (e.g., electrons that have not been observed do not exist, which is a very typical interpretation of the concept "to be means to be perceived (*esse est percipi*)"). Thus, the purpose of science is not to speculate on "the essence of nature" but to "expand our range of experience and summarize those experiences in order." Under this expedient belief, science is reduced to a kind of instrumentalism aiming to guide daily practice and maximize social utilization. In fact, quantum theory has achieved great success under such instrumentalism. Murray Gell-Man, the U.S. Nobel Prize winner, described quantum mechanics as a mysterious and unpredictable subject that no one really understands but just knows how to use. Indeed, that is how quantum mechanics has been applied in life. From computers to washing machines, from mobile phones to nuclear weapons, all these things were made possible with quantum mechanics. The study of quantum mechanics has driven and created the modern world (Kumar, 2012).

Murray Gell-Man's description of quantum mechanics as "mysterious," "unpredictable," and something that "no one really understands" is a view derived from the Uncertainty Principle. That is, an unobserved electron is omnipresent (rather than non-existent) and may appear in multiple places at the same time. However, the electron position is determined once observed. Thus, each observation changes reality, or reality depends on observation. By extension, when observation is not being performed (as in most cases), everything that may occur in the universe is occurring. One thought experiment that extends quantum uncertainty to the macroscopic level is known as "Schrödinger's Cat." In this thought experiment, a cat and a small amount of radioactive material are placed inside a box. There is a 50% probability that the radioactive material will decay and release toxic gas to kill the cat, and a 50% probability that the radioactive material will not decay and the cat will survive. When the box is closed, the entire system maintains a wave state of uncertainty—i.e., the superimposition of the cat being both dead and alive. The fact of whether the cat is dead or alive can be "determined" only after the box is opened and the cat's state is observed by external observers. Advocates of materialism find this concept quite ridiculous, as they hold that objective reality is independent of human will. The cat's state of life or death has already been fixed in advance, as there is only one objective fact. We cannot "discover" (rather than "determine") this fact without opening the box. The so-called superimposition of the cat being both dead and alive is merely the set of all possible states for the cat before the box is opened, rather than the reality itself. Since introduction of the "Schrödinger's Cat" thought experiment, the philosophical view that "to be means to be perceived" has evolved into the statement that "without perception, everything exists." This statement cannot be verified in experiment, as all experiments are processes of perception. However, this perspective still contributes successfully as a theoretical algorithm that can be used to predict many natural phenomena and facilitate many inventions. In conclusion, even if this theory cannot be logically explained, it remains a very successful tool for general application. However, based on its success as a tool alone, we cannot prove the validity of this theory (i.e., that everything that may occur in the universe does in fact occur objectively in the absence of observation).

In some respects, Bohr's view that scientific development should aim to meet the needs of utilitarianism makes sense. All practical activities of mankind must conform to the teachings of utilitarianism, and scientific research is no exception, since science is not otherworldly (as may have been imagined). To understand this, we must distinguish between what is *true* and what is labeled as *truth*. If we say that a cherry blossom petal fallen from a branch in the absence of wind travels 1/3 of the distance from the branch to the ground in the first 5 s, covers another 1/3 of the distance in the following 3 s, and finally reaches the ground in another 2 s, this is true information. Likewise, the description of a loquat leaf falling from a branch in the absence of wind is also regarded as true. So would be the description of the free fall of an iron ball dropped from the Leaning Tower of Pisa. In fact, objective descriptions of all natural phenomena are regarded as being true. Being true is neither scarce nor valuable. On the contrary, the inexhaustibility of true phenomena in life tempts us to refine the "truth" and summarize these conditions once and for all. Truth-seeking is, from its roots, established with a utilitarian purpose. First, truth-seeking yields better adaptation through a deepened understanding of the natural environment. If we can determine the relationship between the falling distance and the elapsed time of a free-falling object, we can make a timely escape before a falling coconut hits our heads. Second, truth-seeking better facilitates transformation of the natural environment. If we can determine the relationship between the falling distance and the elapsed time of a free-falling object, we can create a glider with the longest possible flight time. That is why the formula $h = 1/2gt^2$ (where h, g, and t are height, acceleration due to gravity, and time, respectively) was regarded as the *truth* upon its discovery.

It is generally believed that the utility attribute of truth should follow its truthfulness attribute. That is, regardless of the utilitarian value of a given "truth" in guiding practice, once its fallacies are discovered, it must surrender to the new theory verified as "true" (or at least, having no known fallacies thus far). However, that is not always the case in practice. For example, the Galilean transformation under the framework of Newtonian classical mechanics $x_a = x_b + vt$ (where the final position of object x_a depends on its initial position x_b plus the distance it travels at a certain speed v over a period of time t) has been proven to provide a "rough description" of the positions of low-velocity objects only. In contrast, the Lorentz transformation under the framework of Einstein's theory of relativity $x_a = \gamma (x_b + vt_b)$, with $\gamma = \frac{1}{\sqrt{1-\left(\frac{v}{c}\right)^2}}$, is the "precise description" of all object positions. Nevertheless, the former rather than the latter is popularized in general education for two reasons. First, compared with the easy-to-understand Galilean transformation, one must develop a general understanding of Einstein's theory of relativity to grasp the meaning of the Lorentz transformation; this is challenging for students who do not major in physics. Second, objects encountered in daily life tend to move at low v, which is far smaller than c. In such cases, γ is close to 1 and the Lorentz transformation is approximately equal to the Galilean transformation. Therefore, the simple Galilean transformation can describe the location of objects encountered in daily life with "sufficient" accuracy. Other examples include the once-popular school of psycho-analysis. Though Freud's Psychoanalytic Theory did provide many insights of high perspicacity, it has been all but abandoned in modern psychological practice because psycho-analysis lacks operability and repeatability in practice. In other words, psycho-analysis is closer to an art form, with the therapeutic effect depending on the skill of the psychoanalyst. If a patient happened to encounter an inept analyst casually applying Freud's conclusions, he/she would likely find all his mental illness attributed to childhood trauma or sexual suppression. Hence, the utility attributes of a theory (its ease of understanding and implementation, its scope of application, etc.) have equal—if not more—influence on the acceptance and popularity of the theory as its truthfulness attribute.

Scholars who regard science as instrumentalism tend to accept the idea of "the relativity of truth," as they are either idealists defying the existence of the first tier objective world or agnostics discrediting humans' ultimate ability to comprehend the nature of the first tier objective world. Thus, for them, human observation is confined to the second tier empirical world, and the phenomena being observed depend on the observer's will. Further, their interpretation of the observed phenomena depends on their knowledge preset and educational background at the time. In turn, they realize the futility of pursuing a theory that is absolutely true everywhere and forever because of the inaccessibility of the first tier world. They regard their theories as being destined to be overthrown by usurpers, as the latter apply developed knowledge to expand the former. Scholars will always "stand on the shoulders of giants" to achieve superior interpretations of the same observations, and scientific theories are doomed to go from one "grave" to another. Thus, what remains of scientific research is instrumentalism that can best serve society at the time and maximize its utilization by guiding human practice.

Ironically, scientific theories developed under instrumentalism with the aim of maximizing utility are eventually eliminated because of the great disadvantages of utility. Nicolaus Copernicus once described the responsibilities of astronomers as follows:

> The astronomer's job consists of the following: to gather together the history of celestial movement by means of painstakingly and skillfully made observations, and then—since he cannot by any line of reasoning research the true causes of these movements—to think of and construct whatever hypotheses he pleases such that, on their assumption, the self-same movements, past and future both, can be calculated by the means of the principles of geometry (…) It is not necessary that these hypotheses be true. They need not even be likely. This one thing suffices that the calculation to which they lead agree with the result of the observation. (cited in Austin, 1976, p. 13)

At present, it is understood that no geometric formula of any level of sophistication is sufficiently accurate to predict future trajectories of celestial movement. Instead, we must measure the self-mass of a celestial body and each gravitational field through which it passes, so as to determine the trajectory from the interaction and distortion of the celestial body and these gravitational fields. Likewise, behaviorism, which affirms that psychologists should avoid excessive study of the intractable "black box" of mental activity and focus instead on explicit external behaviors, was once popular in psychology. In detail, behaviorism features the kinds of behaviors that can be retrieved when inputting different stimuli, as well as methods of adjusting input stimuli to control feedback behavior. At present, it is understood that different subjects provide different feedback to even the same input stimulus. This difference is ultimately caused by different microscopic physiological architectures (such as the nervous system structure and the quantity of receptors that respond to a specific stimulus). It is imperative to open the "black box" of mental activities and reveal the reality behind its myths.

Scientific theories developed under instrumentalism often target methods of predicting future events with high probability, but without explaining the internal mechanism. This approach is adopted because of two constraints. First, it is very difficult to find the determinative causal relationship among multiple occurrences that each feature contingent manifestations. Second, a causal relationship may not be applicable for prediction or other practical guidance even if it were identified. Such a probabilistic theory would naturally be replaced by a later theory developed on the basis of causality and the associated mechanism, because of the former's unavoidable shortcoming in terms of result prediction and its ambiguity concerning mechanism explanation. In fact, Einstein evaluated quantum theory as a "transitional" theory with "some rationality." He still believed that "we can build a model of the real world; that is, we can build a theory to reflect the nature of things, not just reflect the probability of an event" (Kumar, 2012, p. 201).

How then should the theories' perspectives developed by scientists who believe in instrumentalism be evaluated? Although those theories are destined to be replaced by later theories (which is more or less accepted by those scientists), a pioneering spirit drove them to perform and direct research under restricted conditions and with limited methods. (Note that the use of probability-based prediction rather than mechanism-based explanation also reflects the limitations of contemporary research methods and indicates that the subject is at an early stage of development.) On the other hand, it should also be noted that the best way to maximize utility is to ignore utilitarianist dogma, such as instrumentalism, during scientific research. The greatest theories in the history of science were usually developed by highly devout scientists who firmly believed that their own theories reflected the "absolute truth." Although it may be impossible to prove either the existence of an objective world independent of human perception or that such a world operates in an orderly manner (Thus, these "truths" are discovered through objectivity, rather than invented through subjectivity.), scientists who believe in the existence of "absolute truth" and the human ability to reveal it demonstrate enthusiasm for their research object (the objective world) rather than the research subject (human welfare) during their scientific practice. Their approach to "truth-seeking" is pure and unadulterated. It is as if one stared into an abyss for a long time until a light appeared to shimmer in the dark, even if the essence of the abyss remained unseen.

Renyuan Dong

EPILOGUE 1
Distant Similarity and Astonishing Conjecture

Core Question: What is the essential structure of the universe?

In Chapter 1, it was conjectured that the universe is not composed of infinite time and space, but rather constitutes the inner body of a giant creature. The nebulas and stars within the universe correspond to the organs and soft tissue of this giant creature. If that is the case, what, then, are humans? The answer is that human beings are essentially parasitic bacteria living within the giant creature. The following questions then arise: Are we probiotics or harmful bacteria? Are natural disasters and environmental changes movements of a universe-generated immune response to human overcrowding and pollution? Moreover, what is taking place in vitro of the giant creature? Perhaps there is another, even larger organism in comparison with which our universe (the giant creature) may be as small as a parasitic bacterium. The structure of nature may thus circulate endlessly...

The reason why human beings cannot equivocate a boundless cosmos with a bounded inner body, and hence cannot associate their stalwart selves with dismissible microbes, is that we lack eyes big enough to behold the universe in one glimpse—nor can we shrink our bodies, as Sun Wukong (the Monkey King) did to enter the body of Princess Iron Fan, and therefore cannot comprehend the world of bacteria inside the human body. Thus, human perception and the study of the external world are hindered if researchers are positioned in a frame of reference of a different magnitude to the objects under observation. However, investigation of various objects and phenomena on macroscopic or microscopic scales can be performed, albeit with extreme difficulty. Hence, astonishing similarities between these items that span distant levels of space and time are recognized, as detailed in Tables Ep 1.1-1.2.

Table Ep. 1.1.
Comparison of The Macroscopic and Microscopic Objects and Phenomena

Macro Level	Micro Level
NGC 4414 Galaxy. Source: The Hubble Heritage Team, NASA (1999)	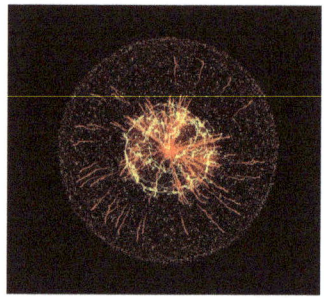 Atom Structure. Source: Media Whale/Dreamstime.
 Tree. Source: Atstock Productions/Shutterstock.	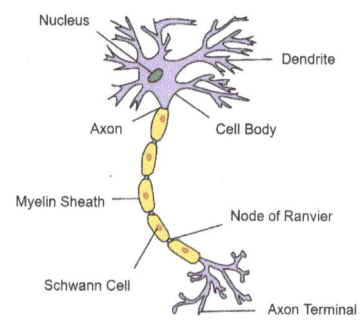 Neuron. Source: Adaptation from US NCI SEER Program (2019)

Table Ep. 1.2.
Comparison of The Macroscopic and Microscopic Objects and Phenomena

Macro Level	Micro Level
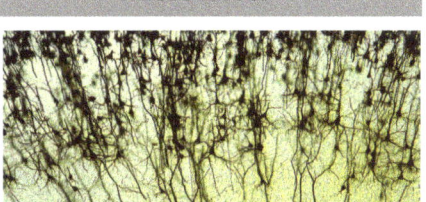 Forest. Source: Vovan/Shutterstock.	Pyramidal neurons in the cerebral cortex. Source: Lange/Shutterstock.
Antimatter has physical properties opposite to matter. Antimatter and matter mutually annihilate to release pure energy upon colliding with each other. However, antimatter is rarely found around the world we live in. The European Space Agency observed a certain region near the center of the universe through a gamma-ray observatory and found a large amount of antimatter. In addition, multiple sources of antimatter have been detected, as antimatter is widely distributed in that conglomeration.	When cells retaining potassium and releasing sodium collaborate with cells retaining sodium and releasing potassium at the resting potential, they can theoretically reach immutability without consuming energy.[7] However, most body cells retain potassium and release sodium at resting potentials, and only glomerular cells distributed in the kidney are subjected to sodium retention and potassium release under the action of aldosterone. For the human body, glomerular cells are as scarce as antimatter in space.

Through the comparison of the macroscopic and microscopic objects and phenomena presented in Tables Ep. 1.1-1.2, one can develop an intuitive sense of the astonishing echoes that reverberate across distant spatial and temporal scales. Some have hinted at the idea of the universe as the body of a giant creature by comparing the human exploration of cosmology in the eye of universe to the same effort made by the ants captive in the manmade colony in the eye of their human breeder:

---

[7] As ions spontaneously flow from areas of high concentration to areas of low concentration, whenever excessive Na^+ must be discharged from a cell after the action potential, those ions are automatically absorbed by nearby cells performing sodium retention and potassium discharge. The Na^+/K^+–ATPase activation is not required during the entire spontaneous process.

Humans used to leave breadcrumbs near the ant nest. Ant theologians discovered this phenomenon and established Bread-Fetishism—bread is God-given and will appear only when one prays devoutly. Later on, humans stopped placing breadcrumbs around their nest, and no matter how devoutly ants prayed, bread never again came out of the blue. The continuous questioning of God's existence gave rise to the Enlightenment, and numerous ant scientists appeared. Ants inspected their own habitat and the glass frame that surrounds it, which they named the Earth and atmosphere, respectively. With time, the ants discovered the larger house that enveloped their habitat—the universe—the light bulb—the Sun—and the switch—the singularity. Eventually, the ants noticed human activities—phenomena that are at times gentle but at others would cause dramatic change to cosmological structural formations, which they called cosmic storms (CME—coronal mass ejection in rigorous academic terms).

The ant scientists summarized these observations into the first principle of the universe: The incidence of cosmic storms are random and unpredictable. The observation of each cosmic storm will lead to different conclusions. The ant scientists summarized these observations into the second principle of the universe: Whenever a cosmic storm sweeps through the singularity (human switches off the light), the Sun vanishes; whenever another cosmic storm sweeps through the singularity (human switches on the light), the Sun reappears. During the solar eclipse, ants learned the light bulb is also coated by a glass cover—the Sun's corona, which was found to be homogeneous across the atmosphere of Earth after careful examination. This finding astonished the scientific community, and some ant scientists raised a bold hypothesis regarding the origin of the universe: The universe used to be a big glass tank. One day, the glass exploded. Some glass shards formed the Sun and some others formed the Earth. However, this hypothesis didn't persuade other scientists because it left unique phenomena, such as cosmic storms and singularities, unsolved.

With more advanced telescopes, ants later discovered the fish tank and thus confirmed the existence of other planets. They discovered the house window and raised the hypothesis that the world is infinite and that other parallel universes may exist. Ants have now discovered the door of the house that is sometimes open and sometimes closed. Ant scientists raised the hypothesis of a black hole and a white hole: When the door opens, the universe opens a black hole. If one goes through the door, he may cross through the white hole into another unknown world on the outside. This hypothesis shakes the world of ants once again. They would say that they were ignorant of the truth of the world, but were endowed with the sense that everything is possible. All they can do is to hypothesize boldly and prove carefully, even though such a validation process is quite ridiculous in the eye of an advanced intelligent creature (adapted from Nmlongyou, 2019).

From the other way around, the concept of the human body as a small universe appears quite often in comics. In the masterpiece *Saint Seiya* by cartoonist Masami Kurumada, a classic line uttered by the main character, Seiya, during a fight is, "Burn, my Cosmo!" Here, "Cosmo" refers to the "small universe" within the gladiator's body, which is composed of atoms with "galactic structures." In that comic, gladiators can use more powerful attack techniques when burning their cosmos (such as the Pegasus Meteor Fist, a comparatively fierce attack technique performed by Seiya), which is somehow consistent with physical principles. According to the Bohr Model that describes the atomic structure in terms of energy levels, electrons release energy when promoted from a ground-state orbit to an excited-state orbit. If gladiators could accumulate this released energy in their fists, they would be able to perform stronger strikes. The burning cosmos concept is the process of energy release by promoting electrons from the ground state to the excited state within one's body, which requires careful control to prevent overloading. Otherwise, the atomic structure collapses, resulting in nuclear fission, which releases unmatched power. Before this power leveled the enemy, it would annihilate the attacker through self-explosion.

It is not claimed that the microscopic and macroscopic structures mentioned above correspond to each other on a one-to-one basis. In fact, it is as difficult to prove that a tree is a neuron in the macroscopic sense and a neuron is a tree in the microscopic sense as it is to falsify that statement. It may be assumed that there are no other similarities between the two entities apart from appearance, whereas the differences are everywhere. For example, the dendrites of one neuron are usually connected to the synapses of another neuron. In contrast, trees stand side by side. The canopy of one tree is rarely connected to the roots of another. One weak explanation is that the trees on Earth can at least be compared to the pyramidal neurons in the cerebral cortex, as illustrated in Table Ep.1.2. The cone system manages skeletomuscular movement and is mainly composed of upper and lower neurons. The upper motor neurons are pyramidal, being arranged in parallel and emitting axons that are bundled into a descending fiber bundle called a pyramidal bundle. This structure is quite similar to that of woodland. The pyramidal neurons are arranged in parallel to construct nerve fiber tissue, and trees stand side by side to form a forest. The axons of pyramidal neurons converge into pyramidal bundles, while the "axons" of trees (their roots) also converge underground to form a large network.

A stronger explanation would be that the major axon-to-dendrite connection pattern between neurons is merely based on our observations of nerve slices under high-power microscopes. (Note that the axon-to-dendrite pattern is selected from among the various neuronal connection patterns, such as axon-to-axon, dendrite-to-dendrite, and axon-to-cell-body.) However, this may not be the real 3D structure of neuronal connections, but rather a 2D projection of the 3D morphology viewed under a microscope.

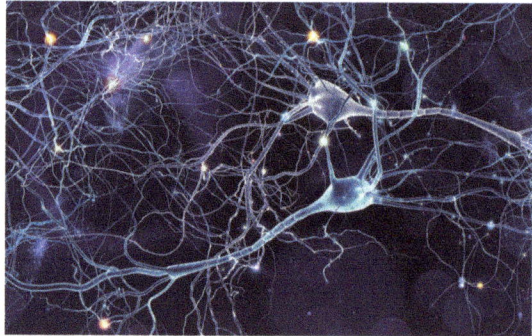

Figure Ep 1.7. Neuron Cell Concept. Source: Whitehoune/Dreamstime.

The common 3D illustration of the nervous system structure is merely a 3D simulation produced by software.

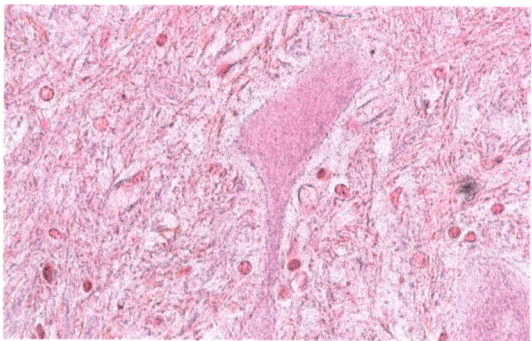

Figure Ep 1.8. Human Nerve under the Microscope. Source: Piyapong Thongdumhyu/Dreamstime.

This is the actual 2D microscopic image of dyed nerve slice observed under high-power microscope.

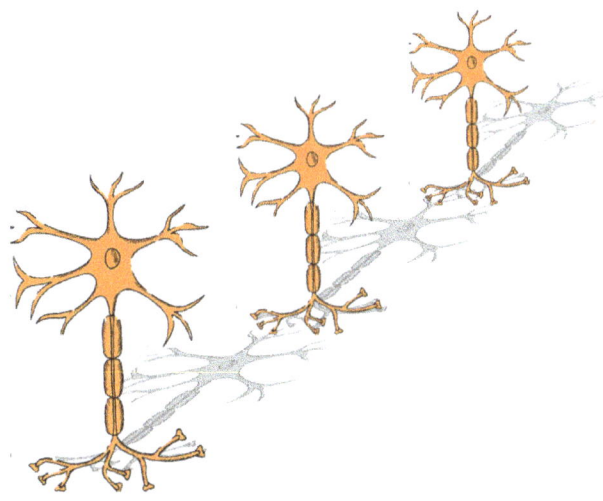

Figure Ep 1.9. Potential Axon-to-Dendrite Neuron Connection Pattern.

This pattern may be a 2D projection image of a 3D morphology in which neurons are arranged in parallel.

Another major difference between a neuron and a tree exists with regard to information transmission. Nerve impulses can only be transmitted unidirectionally from the axon of the previous neuron to the dendrites of the next. However, it is difficult to perceive the kind of information transmitted from one tree's roots to the crown of another. In fact, the answer lies in the carbon dioxide (or carbon) cycle of trees. The roots of one tree absorb oxygen and release carbon dioxide into the soil through respiration at night. During the day, the carbon dioxide retained in the soil is emitted into the air, like a chemical transmitter, as the temperature rises. The canopy of the adjacent tree absorbs this carbon dioxide and releases oxygen through photosynthesis (this oxygen does not easily return to the soil), thereby achieving a directional transfer of information and chemicals. A question may further arise as to why such a relatively long period of time is required for a forest to complete this transmission, which can be completed by neurons instantly. According to the special theory of relativity, time dilates for a high-speed object (its clock ticks slower) from the perspective of a stationary observer, while the distance it traverses is contracted. When a human is stationary relative to a tree and perceives the action potential at a macroscopic level, this transmission of information between neurons is completed without the human's awareness. However, if the human traveled at high speed and remained stationary relative to those electric signals, the decelerated clock would show the proper time, and the contracted length of the neuropathway would restore to its proper length. Thus, from that perspective, the neurons would require a longer period of time to transfer the action potential. Different susceptibilities to the same time periods are therefore developed when traveling through space-time at different velocities.

If trees in the macroscopic world truly correspond to neurons in the microscopic world, we can purposefully verify similar facts for the latter that have already been confirmed for the former, and vice versa. As mentioned in the previous chapter, neurologists discovered that the development of neuronal connections to some extent demonstrates "sociability." Relative to this recent finding, the understanding of the "social behaviors" of plant growth advanced by botanists is even more impressive. Even among plants of the same type, one plant can accurately distinguish its genetic relationship with its neighbors and modify the growth pattern of its roots accordingly. If there is no affinity, the plant extends its roots to obtain as much nutrition as possible. However, if there is an affinity, the plant restrains the expansion of its roots to provide sufficient space for its siblings to grow. A study performed on a cedar forest even revealed that a mother tree sends nutrients, such as carbon and sugar, to a baby tree to support its growth. This transmission is achieved through the fungal root network (Simard, 2016). In a typical virgin forest, the tree roots are entangled with the fungal roots to form an underground "black market." That is, the fungi trade minerals with tree roots for nutrients that they cannot synthesize by themselves, such as carbon and sugar. In the case of breeding offspring, the mother tree can then use fungi as couriers to deliver more nutrients to the soil near the baby tree. If these phenomena also exist in neural network construction, the "social behaviors" of neurons are much more complex than currently supposed. For example, glial cells, which were thought only to function as scaffolding for neurons, may also participate in information exchange (similar to the role of fungi in the example above). Further, the pattern of information transmission may not be simply unidirectional from the axon of the previous neuron to the dendrites of the next neuron.

In summary, if one accepts that there is the possibility of a one-to-one correspondence between many objects and phenomena at the macroscopic and microscopic levels, then depending on his/her beliefs regarding the nature of space-time, either of two major conjectures concerning the essential structure of the universe can be established.

1: If space-time is conceived as boundless and inexhaustible, the human body can be regarded as a small universe; and what we call the universe can also be understood to be the internal body of a giant creature. Outside the universe, there is the "universe" of our universe, i.e., the inside of an even more massive organism... The structure of nature may thus circulate endlessly.

2: If space-time is conceived to have a limited existence with a certain boundary, or even to be a pseudo conception devised by humans to facilitate our understanding of the world, the physical particles observed under a microscope, the humans and plants on the medium scope, and the cosmos and galaxies of the macroscope, actually correspond to the same object groups because of their similarities. That group of objects establishes the "objective world," in which objects are endowed with different velocities to manifest different "time-space illusions," such as different masses, volumes, and elapsed activity times. This is analogous to different distorting mirrors reflecting a varied array of body shapes from one figure. (However, a difference exists in that a distorting mirror can twist the reflected object shapes only through the distortion of the mirror surface, whereas the objective world can distort various object properties, such as their mass, volume, and elapsed time, by manipulating their velocity.) Humans observe these "space-time illusions" from the microscopic to the macroscopic scale, thereby constructing a mental image of the world structured according to space and time.

"If it were not for our conception of weights and measures, we would stand in awe of the firefly as we do before the sun" (Gibran, 1988, p. 52). We can further comprehend the first conjecture from a quantitative perspective, besides the intuitive structural similarities in shape. The radius of the solar system is approximately 122 astronomical units (A.U.; the diameter is approximately 3.6×10^{13} m), while the diameter of the Milky Way is approximately 6.3×10^9 astronomical units (A.U.; the diameter is approximately 9.5×10^{20} m). The difference in the diameter order of magnitude is approximately 2.6×10^7 times. Meanwhile, the average height of the human body is approximately 1.7 m (1.7×10^9 nm), and the diameter of most parasitic viruses is approximately 100 nm. The difference in the diameter order of magnitude is approximately 1.7×10^7 times, which is the same difference level as for the solar system/Milky Way comparison. Likewise, the volume of the solar system is approximately 2.4×10^{40} m^3, based on the assumption that the solar system is a sphere with a diameter of 3.6×10^{13} m (the furthest distance attainable by the solar wind), and the volume of the Milky Way is approximately 6.8×10^{60} m^3, based on the assumption that the Milky Way is a cylinder with a diameter of 100,000 light years and a height of 1,000 light years. The difference in the volume order of magnitude is approximately 2.8×10^{20} times. Meanwhile, the average volume of the human body is approximately 7×10^{25} nm^3, based on the assumption that the human body has an average mass of 70 kg and a density similar to water, which is approximately 1,000 kg/m^3, and the volume of most viruses is approximately 5.2×10^5 nm^3, based on the assumption that the virus is a sphere with a diameter of 100 nm. The difference in the volume order of magnitude is approximately 1.3×10^{20} times, which is the same difference level as for the solar system/Milky Way comparison.

In other words, if we regard the entire Milky Way as the human body, the solar system within is not even sufficiently large to match the size of a body cell but is at most comparable to the virion of a parasitic virus. The multiple planets of the solar system and the various living creatures on those planets are diminished to the organisms and molecules that constitute the virion. Conversely, from the perspective of a virus-sized solar system, other galaxies beyond the Milky Way are equivalent to the bodies of other individuals. Clearly, definite boundaries separating organisms exist (such as the dense skin layer separating an individual's internal body from the external environment); however, those boundaries do not exist from the perspective of a virus. (There are no borders isolating different galaxies, according to current observations.) This is not surprising. Even if skin separates the body spaces of different organisms, the gaps between the skin cells appear large to a virus; therefore, a virion can easily break through to infect neighboring individuals. Similarly, if a spacecraft traveling faster than the fourth cosmic velocity[8] were developed, humans could indeed escape from the Milky Way's gravitational pull, and flight to other galaxies could be realized. Through this comparison, we can hopefully develop a more intuitive sense of the world from the perspective of a microbe living inside the human body.

To grasp the general concept of the second conjecture, one must be acquainted with Einstein's theory of relativity. Some basic and non-mathematical explanations (which are not, in a sense, scientific) of the theory of relativity, and its major principles, are presented below.

Major principles of the special theory of relativity:

1) *Length contraction:* The dimensions (e.g., length) of a fast-moving object as measured by an observer at rest may be smaller than measurements of the same object performed by another observer who is stationary relative to the object.

   As explained with regard to the idiom of "a glimpse of a white horse flashing past a chink in a wall," if a white horse passes by a stationary observer at speed, the latter perceives the horse's body as being shorter than its proper length because of the visual illusion.

2) *Time dilation:* The time lapse between two events is not invariant from one observer to another. The lapsed time of a fast-moving object measured by an observer at rest may decrease as its clock ticks slower.

   It takes an object less time to cover a shorter distance at the same speed. As shown by the example above, as the length of the white horse is measured as being shorter by a stationary observer than by its rider, it passes the stationary observer in less time.

3) *A leading clock lags (relativity of simultaneity):* From the perspective of a stationary observer, a clock decelerates in the direction of the object's movement.

---

8   A cosmic velocity is the minimum speed directed in the necessary direction to escape the gravitational attraction of a cosmic body such as a planet, a star, or a galaxy. E.g. the "first cosmic velocity," known as the orbital velocity, will bring a rocket or other projectile into orbit around the Earth. A slower projectile will fall back to Earth. The "fourth cosmic velocity" is the escape velocity from our galaxy: the Milky Way. It corresponds to about 320 kilometers per second.

Imagine a white horse running at a constant speed through railings aligned with the same interval. The interval between two railings appears shorter the farther away they are situated from the observer because of the perspective relationship. When a white horse gallops away from the observer at a constant speed, it requires increasingly less time to cover seemingly shorter intervals (which are, in fact, the same) from the perspective of the stationary observer. This is as if the clock ticks slower along the direction of movement.

Major principles of the general theory of relativity:

1) *The equivalence principle:* A gravitational field causes the same effects as acceleration. In detail, the dimensions (e.g., length) of a measured object will be shorter, and the time lapse between two events will dilate in a strong gravitational field compared to a weak gravitational field. These length contraction and time dilation effects are enhanced as the gravitational field is strengthened.

    This phenomenon occurs because placement of an object in a gravitational field is equivalent to its placement in an acceleration system. For example, a passenger in a fully enclosed elevator cannot determine whether the elevator is stationary. He is standing on the elevator floor because of the gravitational pull of the Earth, or the elevator is accelerating upwards (in outer space with no gravitational field) and he is standing on the elevator floor because of the reaction force. Therefore, any phenomena that occur with changes in velocity, such as length contraction and time dilation, would also appear in a gravitational field.

2) *Mass-Velocity relationship:* The mass of an object will increase together with its velocity when subjected to an external force or energy supply; in the case of self-energy conservation (without an external energy supply), whenever a stationary object begins to move, it must consume some part of its mass in exchange for velocity by the same principle that rest energy is converted into kinetic.

    The former can be verified by the famous mass-energy equation: $E = \gamma m_v c^2$, where γm_v is the relative mass of the object. The latter can be verified by the transformation $E = mc^2 + 1/2mv^2$.

Einstein's theory of relativity actually indicates that the manifestation of an object's properties, such as its mass and volume, changes when it moves at a high velocity close to that of light or is positioned in a strong gravitational field. In contrast, traditional physics holds that the physical properties of an object always appear constant. This is because humans observe the external world and receive information through light (direct media) or a gravitational field (indirect media). We can always practice steady observations and receive consistent information because light as media travels much faster than most observed objects. (In fact, the relativistic effect is always acting. However, it is too subtle to be noticed most of the time.) Yet, when the speed of the object under observation begins to reach that of the observation media (i.e., the object begins to travel at a speed close to that of light), or when the media itself is distorted (e.g., light bending in a strong gravitational field), the received information changes accordingly. Under these circumstances, the relativistic effect shatters the sensory threshold and manifests itself in intuition.

In order to understand the two conjectures of the essential structure of the universe, especially the second one, we must verify that when a macroscopic object travels at the same velocity as its corresponding microscopic counterpart, the "apparent information" of the former, such as the mass, volume, and elapsed time of motion, is also in accordance with that of the latter (or at least of the same magnitude), and vice versa. Then, we can prove that both objects are merely "space-time illusions" derived from the same objective entity.

Unfortunately, although most microscopic objects travel at high speeds, those speeds are far from that of light. (Of course, we do not exclude the possibility that our measurements are incorrect, as the velocities of many microscopic objects originate from theoretical deduction rather than direct measurement.) Therefore, even if macroscopic objects traveled at the speed of their microscopic counterparts, the relativistic effects of length contraction and time dilation would not be sufficiently significant to unify their "apparent information" (such as the mass, volume, and elapsed time of motion) to the same magnitude as those of their microscopic counterparts. Thus, at present, the credibility of the second conjecture is far lower than that of the first. Space and time remain the stable (in most cases) and objective structures of the world, which accommodates numerous phenomena from the microscopic to macroscopic scale. However, there are astonishing similarities, in terms of physical structure and chemical properties, among objects beholding great differences in their space-time magnitudes, because of the universal characteristics of force interaction and energy transmission. We can use such similarities to speculate on unknown aspects of the universe or even components outside the universe. Whereas quantum theory indicates that "everything that may happen in the universe is happening," this similarity undoubtedly limits the scope of "things that may happen." This is true even for destinations unreached and unknown to human beings. Instead of falling into complete bizarreness and incomprehensibility, happenings there should still exhibit a sense of warmth reminiscent of what we have already experienced. Thus, there is no reason for humans to hesitate at the brink of a step into the "unknown" world and future exploration.

Part Two
Ethics

Renyuan Dong

5

Survival and Reproduction—Another Language for Utilitarianism

Core Question: What Is the Meaning of Life?

All philosophers seek to answer the question of the meaning of life or existence in general. There are two major schools of philosophy that have provided brilliant answers to this question. One is existentialism and the other is utilitarianism. The former claims that "existence precedes essence" (Sartre, 1946/2007, p. 3): the essence of life has no meaning. Each person comes into existence without any purpose. The so-called "meaning of life" is nothing more than a conjecture fabricated by humans so as not to be bored to death throughout the long process of nihilistic existence. The nothingness of life—the essence of nihilism—leads to pessimism about life, just like the Greek parable in Nietzsche's book, *The Birth of Tragedy* (1872/2017). King Midas searched the forest for the wise Silenus and asked him what the best and most desirable thing is for man. Silenus replied with these words: "What is best of all is utterly beyond your reach: not to be born, not to be, to be nothing. But the second-best thing for you—is to die soon" (p. 21). Utilitarianism, on the other hand, asserts that the fundamental meaning of life is to "achieve the greatest good (also called happiness, utility, etc.) for the greatest number." Therefore, behavior that complies with the principle of "gaining advantage and avoiding harm" is not selfish but morally necessary. Integrating the perspectives of these two schools yields the topic of this article: namely, *Existence for Existence's Sake*, which in layperson's terms means the ultimate meaning of present human existence is to ensure that the human race continues to prosper in the future; this is similar to the *will-to-live* proposed by Arthur Schopenhauer.[9] If there were a charter of the *will-to-live*, it would include the following three tenets.

First, reproduce a quantity of high-quality descendants through sexual propagation for the continued existence of the human race.

Second, preserve the present population of high-quality parents in order to achieve future reproduction. For each parent, the present preservation of the whole species is experienced as securing one's own survival and striving for a better life.

Third, help and assist others in society to have better lives after securing one's own welfare, manifested by the combination of egoism and altruism in one's behavior.

However, how does the will-to-live manipulate us through our subconscious without being apprehended and make us behave according to its own will?

First, in order to achieve the initial goal of reproduction, the will-to-live imbues sex with tremendous pleasure to infatuate young men and women of childbearing age with sexual activities. (Studies show that the greatest pleasure a person can experience is sexual pleasure, while the greatest fear is the fear of death.) Children at the rebellious age are often heard quarrelling with their parents, "Did you ever plan for a baby when making love? No! You just indulged in sexual pleasure." Although these words are disrespectful, they are not complete nonsense. Few young couples carry out the mission of reproduction through a sense of responsibility; most are driven by the great pleasure of sex. Yet the natural consequence of sexual activities—the birth of babies—is just what the will-to-live desires. (In modern society, many young adults are urged to marry and bear children as family responsibilities. This was completely unthinkable in primitive tribes, wherein one member of the community would hope the others did not bear children to monopolize the limited resources available for his/her own descendants.)

When we describe the relationship between parents and children in an emotionless language closer to a biological perspective, by removing terms

---

9   The *will-to-live* is a philosophical concept proposed by Arthur Schopenhauer in his work *The World as Will and Representation* (1819/2016), where the *will-to-live* refers to the uncontrollable impulse and unlimited desire for life—namely, survival and reproduction.

such as kinship, family relationship, and bonds of blood, we find that parents are the history of their children, and children are the continuation of their parents. Whenever the human body, as the carrier of the genetic material DNA, starts to age and decay, DNA seeks—or builds, to be precise—a younger, more vigorous body in which to live. Such a process is reflected in the reproductive impulse of human behavior.

Therefore, we as children can be regarded as the resuscitation of the old souls of our parents in young flesh, flesh through which they are able to observe and experience a new world. Likewise, our parents can be regarded as the resuscitation of the even older souls of our grandparents in relatively younger flesh; thus, traces of our grandparents remain in us as the third generation. In this world, there are neither births of new lives nor funerals of old lives. What comes and goes is merely the replacement of the physical carriers. What remains eternal is the genetic material inside.

Of course, breeding and nurturing one's offspring is by no means a casual process. Our parents had to find a person with whom they felt compatible. This is generally referred to as finding "love," a possessor of a DNA library that matches one's own DNA and results in the reproduction of high-quality offspring through the rearrangement and integration of the two sets of DNAs. Our parents then needed to create the best conditions possible for our lives, such as a good education and an environment that safeguarded our health. This is generally referred to as "family responsibilities," the optimized cultivation of the children's innate potential through an acquired environment to ensure that they excel in fierce social competition, which results in the sustainable inheritance of parental genes on to future generations.

The two processes described above are not independent but inseparable. During the time when the importance of genetic roles is stressed, everyone focuses on finding the right person. However, Schopenhauer (1819/2016) believed that the principle of partner selection is no mystery. Everyone endeavors to eliminate their own weaknesses, defects, and deviations from the ideal type through the other individual, lest they be perpetuated or grow into abnormalities in the future child. As de Botton (2000/2004) playfully puts it, "Short women will fall in love with tall men, but tall men will rarely fall in love with tall women (their unconscious fearing the production of giants). Feminine men who do not like sport will often be drawn to boyish women who have short hair (and wear sturdy watches)" (p. 211). Schopenhauer's theory of neutralization is reasonable but not absolute, as in reality we often see compromises: cases wherein someone disregards another's mismatched appearance, temperament, or ability in view of his/her wealth, power, or social status. Epigenetics confirms that the quality of descendants depends not only on the quality of their genes but also on the expression and development level of their innate potential, assisted or hindered by their acquired environment—just as knowing how to play a good hand is as important as having one to win a game of cards. Rich social resources from one's partner would contribute greatly to an environment that provides for the thorough development of a child's innate potential.

Through the entire process of breeding and nurturing offspring, we certainly hope for superiority in the quality of our descendants. More importantly, we (especially males) hope for truthfulness in the genetic relationship between the descendants and ourselves as parents—in other words, that they are our cognations rather than the offspring of some adulterer. We hope that the superior qualities exhibited by our children are faithfully derived from the best expression and rearrangement of our own genes. On the other hand, even if some genes result in features that are rarely regarded as superior but are recognizable enough to leave our imprint/mark on future generations (such as a big forehead or a long face), we would still be able to persuade ourselves to pass on such genes after some inner conflict. Why is that? Why do we pursue the truthful inheritance of genes before superior evolution, even when the inherited genes are not at all superior? There are several reasons. First, the fact that certain genes fail to put one person at an advantage does not mean that the genes are disadvantageous in and of themselves. Their expression may be hindered by incomplete postnatal development. Second, even if one's genes are truly of average quality, they may show new vitality after chromosomal rearrangement through reproduction. In other words, the reason for diversifying the human gene pool is to guarantee heterosis (offspring whose traits are enhanced through the mixing of the parent's genetic contributions), thereby guaranteeing that the human species will continue to prosper. The greater the number of elements for permutation and combination, the more diversified the results of permutation and combination, and the greater the chance of producing high-quality individuals. Humans have no choice but to adopt the mass-production principle based on the possibility of natural evolution until we are able to select and screen our own genes.

As I mentioned at the beginning of this chapter, the ultimate meaning of human existence at present is to ensure one's species continues to prosper in the future. The success of a species' evolution depends not only on its population but also on its position in the food chain. Therefore, we should maintain a population n at all times in history that maximizes the sum of all human capabilities of that population size ($\int_1^n U(x) \cdot dx \rightarrow$ Max, where $U(x)$ is the function representing the capability of each individual, and $\int$ is the integral accumulating all the individual capabilities of population n). That formula suggests an alternative to the long-held belief that group *capacity* could grow only through an increase in the population: recent advances in science and technology mean that group capacity can also be increased through greater individual ability within the same population, thus freeing humans from mass production. In ancient agrarian society, the tribe with the greater population was usually the victor in war, notwithstanding some victories against the odds. When it comes to modern warfare, however, one soldier armed with modern military weapons can battle against a hundred primitive soldiers with spears. Driving up overall capacity by enlarging the population is inefficient and will eventually reach an upper limit. Instead, enhancing the ability of each individual is a better choice than the big-crowd strategy, as it gives each member a premium—more resource allocation per capita and consequently a greater sense of satisfaction—while achieving the same overall effect as the latter. Thus, with the ultimate goal of achieving the sustainable reproduction of the human species remaining unchanged, the direction of social development and human practice has shifted from "mass production" to "god creation" (or at least, superman creation) for the first time in history.

Genetic screening and genome editing make "god creation" possible in the future. Once genetic screening and genome editing have been sufficiently developed to eliminate any risks, the former will certainly become more acceptable to the public from an ethical perspective. Genetic screening would allow for the selection and fertilization of the best individual sperm and ovum from the numerous copies provided by my partner and me, thus achieving optimal reproduction from the limited possibilities of our mating. The superior qualities of our children still originate from our individual genetic material. Suppose that one day, all males and females of childbearing age are required to disclose their genetic maps. You would not need to look for a mate in the crowd; the local medical center would search in the global database and find you the "right person," the person whose DNA perfectly matched with yours to produce descendants of the finest possible quality. He/She might live on the other side of the earth, and you two would have never met in the past. There is still no need for you to waste time meeting in person even now. All you need to do is take your sperm/ovum out of your body, freeze it, and send it to a certified institute for reproductive health, where your future baby will thrive in a test tube.

Who should raise the baby after its birth? Do not forget that a child's finest qualities cannot be cultivated without adequate postnatal upbringing to nurture the child's innate potential, and the analysis from the database shows that neither of you are fit for the job of parenting. If the child were raised by you, its potential might be wasted. Do not worry; your child will be taken care of by a group of "professional parent agents"—a new, well-paid profession—who are especially good at raising children. What would be the next step for you and your partner? "Of course, to continue pursuing your own dreams! The biggest advantage of this technology is to liberate the rest of your life from the burden of childbearing to allow for the fulfillment of your own self-worth, isn't it?" excitedly explains a project manager of genetic screening. You might think that such reproductive technology and processes have already greatly violated your parental rights, while the genome editing could provide you with an even more amusing scheme.

The technology of genome editing at present has a limited capability to add in or knock out specific DNA fragments to or from genomes. It will reach maturity once any base pair at any position on the DNA double helix can be rearranged at will to optimize the phenotype of an individual. By then, scientists will have clarified the correspondence between the modification of a DNA fragment at a specific site on the double helix and an improvement in a particular observable characteristic or internal ability. Once all 23 pairs of chromosomes have undergone such a retrofit, the "crystallization of human wisdom" literally comes into being. How dare we consider ourselves to be the parents of the "child of God," who far surpasses his/her precursors in appearance, physique, wisdom, and every other feature? We know clearly that this child of God could be born from the sperm and ovum donated by my partner and me, just as he/she could be born from the sperm and ovum donated by the couple next door. In fact, he/she could be born from the sperm and ovum donated by any healthy couple with 23 pairs of chromosomes composed of purine and pyrimidine pairs. We are all reduced to mere suppliers of the raw material. Regardless of the quality of the raw material, science and technology will retrofit and improve every gene of the child to the point of perfection. If this child of God has parents, their names would be science and technology.

The maturity of genome editing will pose enormous challenges to ethical values in today's society. First, "truthful inheritance" is no longer a principle that we must abide by in the process of reproduction. The child born from our sperm and ovum can no longer be called "our child," since genetic retrofitting has effaced his/her genetic similarity with his/her precursors. Second, we are freed from the burden of natural sexual propagation, as the creation of any *homunculus* would undergo a process of extraction from the parent's body, *in vitro* fertilization, *in vitro* genomic editing, and embryogenesis in an artificial medium. Last, there is no need to preserve a large population as at present, because diversifying the human gene pool to guarantee heterosis is no longer a necessity. We do not need to adopt mass production and rely on nature to breed and screen for high-quality descendants. In theory, humans only need one Adam and one Eve to supply the raw material; thereafter, we can rely on the "hand of science" instead of the no longer unfathomable "hand of the creator" to carry out targeted improvements to our genes based on our needs, such as customizing a poet of peerless sentiment, a scientist of unparalleled intelligence, an athlete of unrivaled strength, etc.

Any of the three statements above are deviant from today's perspective; humans tend to hold inexplicable fears and suspicions about the unknown, especially when technology is in its infancy. Though ethical discussions about a technology that will mature over centuries undoubtedly makes overly advanced demands on modern citizens in terms of our acceptable range of ideas for debate, we must not forget that ethical values about humanity will evolve along with society and its technologies. Let us suppose that, by the time genome editing matures, the moral standard of humans has evolved to such a degree that we are willing to cede control of the future to the homunculus (or neo-human) created by us. The only concern would be whether we can bid farewell to this world with dignity. On what basis can we assert that we will not be the next gorillas viewed in the zoo? Further, on what basis can we assert that we won't be enslaved as the intelligent robot cleaners of the next generation?

The Japanese anime *From the New World* depicts a future where neo-humans coexist with their livestock of monster rats. The neo-humans in that world do not demonstrate a huge evolutionary leap from the condition of today's humans. Their only specialty lies in their psychic abilities that enable telekinesis and—to a certain degree—the manipulation of shockwaves, which are quite humble abilities compared to those conjured in other animations featuring superpower themes. Since psychic abilities make the killing of one another easier, the neo-humans introduce a death mechanism to their own code of behavior for social stability—specifically, if a psychic human kills another, a biological death feedback is activated that causes the murderer's organs to shut down and the attacker to die almost instantaneously. The neo-humans, who have achieved internal peace, enslave the mole-like monster rats, which appear to be obedient to humans but are deceitful in nature. The anime primarily tells the story of how the monster rats, unable to bear their slavery, pursue an ill-fated rebellion against the humans. It ends with a scene where human representatives sit in the military tribunal awaiting the verdict for the mastermind of the monster rats. When the defendant bellows, "We are the humans instead!" the audience bursts into laughter. What the neo-humans who ridicule this statement don't know is that the monster rats are the descendants of those humans who failed to awaken their superpowers in the past. In ancient times, humans with superpowers had forced those without powers to interbreed with naked mole rats in order to eradicate the human appearance of their offspring—the monster rats of today. They did so willfully to misrule them through their psychic abilities without triggering the biological death feedback.

No one can help but gasp at this part of the story. Some may still regard it as an exaggerated concern about the future derived from those inexplicable fears and suspicions about the unknown. However, once you recall the catastrophic extermination our ancestor Sapiens visited on other archaic humans, such as the Neanderthals, or the degradation of our brothers and sisters simply because of the color of their skin, you will find this dystopian story terribly realistic.

There are three ways to protect the humans of today from the slavery of neo-humans in the future. First, every phenotype of the human body depends on the coordinated expression of multiple genes. Almost all the features that humans care about, such as height, appearance, intelligence, and athletic ability, are controlled by hundreds or even thousands of genes. It will be infeasible to edit and modify such a large number of genes simultaneously for a long time in the future. Moreover, how should we modify these genes? "Some individual genes have a good version and a bad version. While the good version functions normally, the bad version leads to diseases. Our current genome editing technology for medical purpose aims to change the bad into the good, thus preventing the occurrence of diseases. However, things are not that simple for features such as height or intelligence. There is neither a 'dwarf' gene nor a 'fool' gene to retrofit, as each gene is responsible for multiple tasks. Even determining whether one gene is good or bad is difficult, not to mention understanding how good or how bad the gene is" (Ent_evo, 2017, n.p.). There is still much to be done to reveal the unfathomable hand of the creator. However, even at present, there seems to be no obstacle barring us from one day understanding the co-operative mechanism of the entire genomic system.

Second, we could elevate the moral standards of neo-humans so they will not repeat the mistakes of our ancestors. "Just as the Atlantic slave trade did not stem from hatred toward Africans, but indifference to their fate, so the modern animal industry is not motivated by animosity; again, it is fueled by indifference" (Harari, 2017, p. 323). The key to improving morality lies in the elimination of such indifference, caused by alienation and instrumentalism, to ensure that neo-humans treat their precursors as their own compatriots. In any case, the humans of today would inevitably retreat to less important social areas with the rise of neo-humans, due to the significant gap in capabilities between the two. Thus, human authority would perish and discrimination against humans would follow.

Last, the birth of neo-humans will also require a thorough postnatal upbringing to release their innate potential. Even if the mystery of genes is revealed, the question of how to create a living environment to optimize the potential of neo-humans remains. The trial-and-error exploration of suitable childcare may be dominated by the humans of today but would be gradually taken over by neo-humans as time passes.

The number of humans of today will inevitably decrease in the future, but we may avoid the fate of enslavement through the three strategies set out above, eventually ceding this world to the neo-humans, who will have evolved and mutated from us, with the help of science, in a progressive manner.

Renyuan Dong

6

Is Happiness More Important Than Anything Else in Life?

Core Question: What are the Similarities and Differences between Utilitarianism and Hedonism?

In the opening chapter of *An Introduction to the Principles of Morals and Legislation*, Jeremy Bentham (1823) states that, "Nature has placed mankind under the governance of two sovereign masters, pain and pleasure" (p. 1). The incentive for human behavior is not the pursuit of evolution, but simply to seek pleasure and avoid pain. However, this instinct to gain advantage and avoid harm invariably results in an increase in human capabilities, which is in line with the continuous and prosperous reproduction of the human species directed by the will-to-live. We do not imagine that, in primitive tribes that lived by hunting and gathering, our ancestors gathered around and agreed on a policy that each community member must master the technique of fire lighting from thence forward as a means to extrude the beasts and thereby ascend the throne of the prairie. It is most likely that the technique of fire lighting was accidentally discovered by a community member, and the lucky dog used the technique to successfully hunt and cook a wild boar for a big meal; this was enough to make him happier than his hungry compatriots. He generously shared the remains with other community members (since there was no refrigeration at the time); this made him the prototype of Prometheus, who brought fire to humankind, in the eyes of others. Their respect, coupled with his promotion in the tribe, made him even happier. What about the other ambitious males who coveted the throne of the tribal chief? They were haunted by a feeling of inferiority due to their less honorable position than the discoverer of fire, and their resolve to rid themselves of the feeling of inferiority made them devoted to practicing the technique of fire lighting as well—whether by humbly asking the pioneer for coaching or by learning secretly from peeping and eavesdropping. By the time the entire tribe had mastered the technique of fire lighting, little sparks were powerful enough to light great fires on the prairie, and humans had replaced lions at the top of the food chain.

Similarly, it is not likely that elders in an agricultural society would assemble the whole family to set a more ambitious goal for a year's food production than those of nearby families solely to establish the family's fame and prestige. It is more likely that one household worked hard one year and harvested sufficient grain for basic food and clothing, as well as surpluses that they could exchange for jewelry made from seashells. Their relative opulence compared to other households in the extended family made them happier. Meanwhile, their neighbors began to increase the scale of their planting to rid themselves of their sense of relative poverty, which made them feel bad, thus introducing competition in food production into the family. Consequently, the whole family became the richest village by the following year, with grain production that was unparalleled for hundreds of miles, even without economic planning.

As we can see, pleasure or pain is generated from a feeling of relative superiority or deprivation when one compares oneself to others, where the object of comparison (the imaginary enemy) is not another distant species or race but rather another close member of the same community. One is happy when one has more than others have and is miserable when falling behind. The will-to-live employs *the pleasure principle* to guide the natural human instinct of pleasure-seeking to enhance overall human capabilities by the following mechanism: A human pursues happiness → the only route to happiness is to be superior to others → the only way to be superior is to enhance one's ability and excel in social competition → others feel miserable due to their relative inferiority to the leader → they work hard to match their abilities to that of the leader in order to get rid of the pain → overall human capabilities improve. The social competition has resulted in a draw, which cancels out the original happiness and pain → whoever wants to be happy again needs to further enhance his/her ability.

However, comparison doesn't just arouse self-motivation. Trying to keep up with the Joneses also results in behaviors such as jealousy, defamation, plunder, and usurpation, as "debasement is the password of the base" (Bei, 1990, p. 33). Compared with other painstaking efforts, it is also possible to plunder the reputation and social status of others by cajolery, and to usurp the wealth and social resources of others by coercion. Is such reaping without sowing utilitarianism's more efficient approach to happiness? In the *Grounding for the Metaphysics of Morals*, Kant (1981) states that one is to "act only in accordance with that maxim through which you can at the same time will that it become a universal law" (p. 30).

Let us imagine what a society that allowed jealousy, defamation, plunder, and usurpation would be like. Obviously, everyone would take these easy approaches and abandon traditional hard work. Thus, there is no reputation to be ruined if everyone chooses defamation instead of building his/her own reputation. There is no wealth to be plundered if everyone opts for looting instead of accumulating his/her own wealth. Such a society would automatically perish through self-destruction. Therefore, even though these despicable practices conform to the interests of some rule-breakers, they are doomed to fall out of the scope of universal laws.

The will-to-live introduces *the reality principle*, as opposed to *the pleasure principle*, and prevents the behavior from becoming universal. The reality principle stipulates that one must compromise one's self-interest when personal desire violates the rights of others in order to maximize society's collective interest. This principle is often adopted when social moral codes and legislative norms are designed. Both principles are based on utilitarian considerations, but the latter calculates the utility across the entire society.

Today, we observe public moral codes and laws so voluntarily that we hardly feel the impact of the reality principle. However, any ethical or altruistic behavior is not *a priori* but more akin to conditioned reflexes so proactive and automatic as to almost delude us about the original goodness of human nature—as if humankind is born with such high moral standards. The American psychologist Kohlberg divides human moral development into three levels: pre-conventional, conventional, and post-conventional. Moral judgments at the pre-conventional stage are decided by the consequences of the behavior; morality at the conventional stage conforms to the expectations of others and to social moral codes; and people make moral judgments at the post-conventional stage according to their own personal will, obeying their chosen moral principles.

Kohlberg's theory is similar to behaviorism's account of the formation of conditioned reflexes. The necessary elements for classical conditioning are the response behavior; the unconditioned stimulus that unconditionally, naturally, and automatically triggers the response; the conditioned stimulus that eventually triggers a conditioned response once it is associated with the unconditioned stimulus; and the repetition of the conditioned stimulus, which enhances and preserves the conditioned response behavior in the long run. Pre-conventional morality is simply the formation of the conditioned reflex. Let us look at a common social scenario, such as an elder boarding a full bus. Upon seeing the elder scanning the aisles in a vain search for an empty seat, one may feel an urge to give up his/her own seat (response behavior), for which he/she may receive praise (unconditioned stimulus). The repetition of this scenario solidifies the connection between the two events such that an elder getting onto a bus becomes the conditioned stimulus, and one's standing up to offer a seat becomes an automatic response (conditioned reflex). At the second developmental level (conventional morality), one figures out that praise is not for the specific act of giving one's seat to the elder but rather for the norm of respecting elders that underlies the behavior. Individuals at this stage would change their behavior in response to different conditioned stimuli (different social scenarios when encountering elders), while the norm of respecting elders that sits behind the various responses remains the same. People conform to the social order and others' expectations in the pursuit of more unconditioned stimuli: rewards and praise. This phase is also the generalization process of a specific conditioned stimulus. At the stage of post-conventional morality, people do not only modify their behavior in response to different conditioned stimuli but also become indifferent to external unconditioned stimuli; that is, they still act to respect elders in different social scenarios without rewards because the norm of respecting elders has itself become a part of their moral code. The persistence of their behavior does not rely on the external repetition of unconditioned stimuli, such as rewards or penalties, but on self-reinforcement. People at this stage act for their inner peace of mind. As different acts to respect elders comply with their own moral code, their performance manifests their free will. This phase is also the internalization process of the external unconditioned stimulus. Individuals of superior morality have reached the third level, where they act in accordance with their internal ethics rather than for utilitarian purposes. However, we must not forget that any morality develops from the lower to the higher level and, at the initial stage of pre-conventional morality, any behavior is in line with the principle of gaining advantage and avoiding harm. Thus, all later moral codes are essentially derived from the tenets of utilitarianism.

You may have already realized through reading the preceding discourse that there is no significant increase in the level of human happiness, despite ever-increasing human capabilities and an ever-evolving society. It is generally believed by historians that members of agricultural societies had a lower level of happiness on average than their counterparts in primitive tribes. At first, farmers on arable land thrived in comparison with migrants; therefore, the few settled farmers appeared to be happier than the large number of migratory hunter-gatherers. However, such relative superiority disappeared as more and more hunter-gatherers joined the group of settled farmers. Further happiness could only be generated when the food production of one household surpassed that of its neighbors; given that all members of a community had access to similar farming technologies, the number of laborers played a decisive role in whether or not this relative abundance was reached. Each household therefore began to have more offspring, which resulted in greater food production in total but fewer social resources per capita than in primitive hunter-gatherer societies. This situation is known as the luxury trap. "One of history's few iron laws is that luxuries tend to become necessities and to spawn new obligations. Once people get used to a certain luxury, they take it for granted. Then they begin to count on it. Finally, they reach a point where they can't live without it" (Harari, 2017, p. 84).

Humanity's search for an easier life released immense forces for change that transformed the world in ways nobody had envisioned or wanted. In fact, as long as one agrees that pleasure or pain is generated from the feeling of relative superiority or inferiority compared with other social members, a society's overall happiness is largely a zero-sum game at any point in history—whenever there are winners, there must also be losers. The suppressed feeling of relative deprivation, exacerbated by polarization between the rich and the poor in today's society, may eventually result in violent conflict. Meanwhile, the happiness of the leader will not last long. The will-to-live may grant us a sweet but short-lived reward when our ability exceeds that of others, but such happiness will *vanish* into the wind as soon as the surrounding world catches up with us. It is noteworthy that I used the word vanish rather than sink, as we can only experience short-term happiness—a temporary emotional fluctuation drawn upward by competitive advantage at the time when our ability has improved. The level of long-term happiness, however, would not accumulate in line with the gradual progression of our abilities, but reset to its original level whenever the outcome of social competition returns to a draw.

Our pursuit of happiness is bound to a tragic destiny just like the myth of Sisyphus. Our muscles (our abilities) have been well developed in the endless process of rolling the boulder up the steep hill, yet the pleasure of achieving the goal, and the sense of accomplishment, always perishes instantaneously as the boulder rolls back down to the bottom. "In that case, we should follow the doctrine of God," some transhumanists propose. "The goal of our life is to constantly increase our knowledge and ability instead of being trapped in frivolous feelings." "No, just the opposite," say others. "We should no longer be manipulated by the will-to-live, but pursue happiness to the greatest degree possible at the current level of competence." The conflict between the two is the fundamental difference between utilitarianism and hedonism—happiness as a means to evolution (which can therefore be abandoned) vs. happiness as the ultimate goal. The vast majority of people tend to vacillate between these two positions. We want to enjoy both happiness and success/achievement (which requires hard work), preferably in the most effortless manner possible. We would definitely have less fun and experience less happiness if the road to success were tremendously painstaking.

Such paradoxical daydreams of "winning easily to maximize happiness" are often demonstrated through thought experiments. On the one hand, one can easily "have it both ways" by attaching value to the areas one is good at and in which it is easy to excel, thus removing value from arduous pursuits ill-suited to his/her predisposition; one wouldn't feel the least sense of regret, even if it entails a loss within the mainstream competition, since those areas are intentionally ignored and devalued. On the other hand, one may worry that such happiness is just self-delusion and still wish that his/her superiority could be widely recognized by mainstream society. Therefore, is the state of happiness, and similar concepts such as pleasure, beauty, and value, just a subjective judgement in accord with one's own heart? In other words, can what I think is happiness essentially be happiness as long as I can persuade myself of the belief? Or is the state of happiness grounded in an objective frame of reference universally acknowledged in society? In other words, does true happiness come from others' surrender to one's superiority and quenching the thirst for adoration from the crowd? Once again, the vast majority tend to vacillate between the subjective and objective natures of happiness.

There was once a debate on the talk show *U can U BiBi* on the topic[10]: if there were a button that could customize a perfect life for your child, would you as the parent press this button? One of the mentors on the show pointed out that if this button could bring a charmed life to the child, the parent might wish to try it (Ma, 2017). The so-called charmed life refers to the fantasy wherein the child is born to a carefree family, without ever knowing hunger; he/she then grows into a mediocre student who can still catch up with the class; difficulties at work and in love may be encountered at first, but there would always be a happy ending waiting ahead... Such supplications for the child, commonly made by parents at religious ceremonies, are ardent—but pigs might fly. A good life deserves to be fought for. Today, you wish a life for your child that is smiled upon by fortune and not necessarily commensurate with his/her deserts. What does such a wish steal? It robs the good life and social resources that are supposed to be distributed to those aiming high and striving hard. There is still a trace of delusion in such a wish; well, wish on!

However, if you try to make such delusions a reality by pressing a button, you have already exposed your greediness to earn a reward for no effort. Even the seemingly selfless cry of, "All for my child!" cannot conceal your avaricious nature. It is not that someone would accuse you of disrupting social justice and fairness when you attempt to do this, but that the wonderful things that you wish for would not be realized at all. Even if there were such a button today, many more people than you would wish to press it. What might happen if everyone tried to own the button? In a civilized society, the button would be auctioned off and command such an extremely high price that only the wealthiest person could afford it, a person whose child has already benefited from an initial generous allocation of resources. A further blessing of good fortune would lead to a growing wealth gap between different social classes. If the poor realized that they stood no chance of beating the rich at auction, they might seek to obtain the button by plunder or theft. Either way, civilized or violent, using the button could eventually result in a breach of social peace.

If there were a button created for ensuring a good life for a child through the blessings of fortune, it would very likely trigger the avarice of the masses. To make things worse, such avarice may be rationalized under the seemingly selfless cover of, "All for the child." I have no idea who would press the button in the end or whose destiny it would change, but I do sus-

---

10 *U can U BiBi* is a talk show in China that focuses on debate. This topic comes from the 16th episode of Season 4.

pect that Pandora's box would be opened as people fought for the button with eager desire.

Designing the operating mechanism behind the button to manage and control the destiny of the child presents another difficulty. The only feasible way I could think of before running out of ideas was to create a real-life version of *The Truman Show*. There would be no safer means than writing the entire life of the child into a script in order to fully control every detail and exclude all uncertainties. In the movie, Truman discovers various absurdities and loopholes in Seaheaven Island; initially unbeknownst to him, the island is the set of a show that actually serves tens of thousands of TV watchers rather than the protagonist himself. That is why the crew sprays artificial rain only over his head to save costs; that is why his wife speaks farfetched lines in order to insert advertisements; that is why his father, who should have died from drowning, attempts to return to the show for some extra episodes... Here, you press the button and a boat will take your child to New Seaheaven Island, where the child won't be stared at or discussed by the crowd. No one on the island is an actor who can accidentally let the cat out of the bag. They are all humanoid AI robots programmed to serve your child with a good life, the instructions to which might include the deliberate creation of some small difficulties or frustrations for your child to overcome, thus helping him/her to achieve personal growth and a sense of accomplishment.

Except by accident, your child would never find out that this is an artificially designed utopia. Is this world real in the child's eyes? Quite real. Are the child's actions free of constraints? Very free. Is the child's life happy? Extremely happy. This is the cognitive dilemma described by the brain in a vat.[11] According to such stories, the computer sending signals to the brain in the vat would be simulating reality and the "disembodied" brain would continue to have perfectly normal conscious experiences without their being related to objects or events in the real world. The subject in a world can never justify his/her cognition of the world from God's perspective (the objective perspective of a third party) because he/she is always captive to his/her own subjective perspective. In this remake of *The Truman Show*, the only one who has God's perspective is you, the parent, who deliberates over whether to press the button.

---

11 The brain in a vat describes a scenario where a mad scientist removes a person's brain from his/her body, suspends it in a vat of life-sustaining liquid, and connects its neurons via wires to a supercomputer that provides it with electrical impulses identical to those the brain normally receives. It is an updated version of René Descartes' evil-demon thought experiment ideated by Gilbert Harman.

If you still regard such a life as good, then you in fact think that there is nothing more important than subjective feelings throughout one's life. "For a man, the most important thing is to be happy." Oh dear, I won't force you to change your view, but I will request you play the role of a good parent really well. Yes, there is still one role left on New Seaheaven Island that needs to be played by a human—the parent who pretends not to know the truth. You must try hard to forget that there is a real world outside this utopia, a broader sky beyond the horizon of this artificial island; you must not let your children suspect that their parents have been hiding something from them all the time. Your child is born as a caged bird who does not see the prison. The one who feels imprisoned is you, who once soared through the blue sky.

As long as you feel the slightest sense of ridiculousness or pity about such a life, you agree that the good life should, in fact, meet some of the criteria of widely accepted social values where objective reality and freedom are indispensable elements. There is a famous question, "Is it better to be a Socrates dissatisfied or a pig satisfied?" Those who ask the question are all potentially Socrates. Pigs are ignorant of superior beings like the dissatisfied philosopher. Everyone wants to be a philosopher, yet most are intimidated by the pains and frustrations of philosophical studies. Those who long to be philosophers but dare not, and are thus left with no alternative but to remain pigs, will not be pigs truly satisfied. One's desire naturally expands after seeing a more advanced life form, while one's cowardice is exposed, since he/she dare not shoulder the pains along with the evolution. The frustration brewed from the fight waged between the two will be deeply etched in his/her heart, no matter how hard he/she tries to forget the existence of philosophers in the world. True happiness always belongs to the ignorant frog[12] at the bottom of a well before it jumps out, since we instinctively aspire to explore the broader world once we know of its existence. This innate, enterprising spirit has made us the overlords of the Earth today.

Of course, subjective feelings and the diverse values of each individual have gained a more widespread respect nowadays. You have been bruised and wounded by life. You have failed to achieve socially defined successes in life even though you have tried hard. You are tired now. You want to let go of yourself. You wish to break free from the life where you were kidnapped by the enterprising spirit. You sighed to yourself and said, "For

---

12 A Chinese fable says that one always shows off its geographical knowledge in front of others, yet it is simply an ignorant frog at the bottom of a well who mistakes the little patch of sky above for the whole world.

a man, the most important thing in life is to be happy." I wish you would say the same to your children when they fall over, when they get hurt, and when they fail to achieve what they aim for, rather than hurrying to immerse your children in the "honey pot" for fear of injury when they are just born and have barely had the chance to experience the sweetness and bitterness of life.

7

The Conformity to Utilitarianism by Anti-Utilitarian Events and the Violation of Utilitarianism by Utilitarian Events

Core Question: How is the Unity of Opposites Demonstrated in Utilitarianism?

Utilitarianism is not as simple as the principle of "gaining advantage and avoiding harm." In contrast, the precise calculus of the happiness and pain of an entire society is so complex that it has spawned a separate discipline of economics. In reality, we often find that the behavior of people who thirst for quick success and instant rewards departs from the doctrines of utilitarianism, while other behavior that is seemingly absent of desires complies with the teachings of utilitarianism in unexpected ways.

Evolutionary humanism, or transhumanism, would be increasingly powerful if utilitarianism were solely about gaining advantage and avoiding harm. Evolutionary humanism follows the logic of Darwinism and considers it necessary to eliminate unqualified individuals through natural selection, or artificial selection in the radical sense, for fear that people will degenerate into sub-humans otherwise. It is only through ensuring that future generations have superior qualities that the human species will evolve into the "superman" (adapted from Harari, 2017). The core of evolutionary humanism coincides with the will-to-live in its search for high-quality descendants through natural reproduction (or even designing neo-humans through science and technology), except for the fact that evolutionary humanism is less tolerant of vulnerable groups. It affirms that vulnerable groups should be deprived of their right to life since their existence is a waste of resources and poses a potential threat to reduce the quality of the entire human species. Nazism was a noxious apostle of evolutionary humanism that promoted white supremacy and slandered other "inferior" ethnicities, such as Jews, who tarnished the noble Aryan ancestry. Modern genetic studies, however, have proved that the differences between genetic lineages of different ethnicities are too negligible to distinguish the superior from the inferior. The fundamentalism of evolutionary humanism should make some sense when we separate it from the wrongdoings of Nazism; otherwise, the oblique evolutionism, by roundabout means, would not have been preserved throughout history, even though the aggressive evolutionism pursued through massacres has not survived.

The most important reason why the bloodthirstiness of aggressive evolutionism did not survive does not lie in the ridiculousness of its theory, but in its complete lack of feasibility. How should we distinguish the superior from the inferior? Through testing? We can design an examination to test people's abilities comprehensively, including intellect, morality, physical wellness, etc., where those reaching the average level and above would be stamped as accepted products while the rest would be disposed of as defective products by the manufacturing assembly line. How much weight should be assigned to each capability in this test? Every one percent increase in the weight of physical-education scores is large enough to allow many with all brawn and no brain to take the place of bookworms who are poor at sports and vice versa. Designing a capability test that is objective and fair alone has already made policymakers tremendously cautious. Furthermore, the world has both child geniuses who run out of wits later in adulthood and late bloomers who struggle in their childhood. At what age should individuals be tested to assess their lifelong potential correctly, without overestimating or underestimating their future contribution? With that in mind, who should take the exam? There is no doubt that infants and elders are the most vulnerable age groups. Infants could be spared the tests until their potential is fully developed. What about elders? Most of the infirm of yesteryear would not escape the fate of elimination. Would the vast majority in their adulthood still endorse such a test, given that the elders' fate today will be the newcomers' future?

Finally, even if the problems set out above were solved and humans were divided into the qualified and the defective, are you still indulging in the wild idea that this is a war between these two groups? Imagine you, the parent, are stamped as accepted while your child fails the exam. Would you place righteousness above family loyalty? Could you abandon your child—the continuation of your genes into the future? If not, then there would be more and more "superior" members joining the camp of the "inferior" members out of consanguinity or sympathy. Moreover, even if the qualified members eventually managed to eliminate the defective members, would the "purified world" be free of discrimination against the fool? Of course not! Those hidden crowds who barely passed the cut-off line and could have been the pot calling the kettle black would immediately be exposed as the new target of social discrimination; even worse, they would be the potential target for the next purge when there are no weaker groups left. Thus, those with crisis awareness would form a united front with the defective group out of their own future interest rather than for the benefit of the latter. The fight would eventually evolve into a battle between a handful of elites with radical views and the vast remainder of the population. The bloody conflict that aggressive evolutionism leads to will never occur out of utilitarian and practical considerations, as no one is sufficiently stupid to start a war that is destined to fail—the outcome of the war would be long anticipated/envisioned before it even began.

However, the discussion above about the design of the examination looks very familiar. We do design various school-entrance exams and job interviews in accordance with similar rules in real life. Meanwhile, we find that a single test is insufficient to reveal candidates' lifelong potential. At most, it can indicate their capability for the next few years. Therefore, we create processes to retest them and update the results at each turning point in their life. Oblique evolutionism, with its many byways, has been preserved all the while. This doesn't deprive vulnerable groups of their right to life, unlike aggressive evolutionism. However, it invests less educational resources in the vulnerable, forces them to take trivial jobs with little pay, and makes them struggle with limited social resources and a strong sense of relative deprivation. Surprisingly, this time everyone agrees with the rules of the game and regards them as fair and justified.

However, this does not mean that the shadow of aggressive evolutionism has vanished. How many malformed fetuses or newborns with major congenital diseases are aborted or abandoned by young couples at medical institutions, leaving them to perish unattended? The rapid economic growth of the United States since 1973 is sometimes considered inextricably linked with the right to legal abortion conferred in the Roe vs Wade case in the same year. Many people believe that the demand for abortion usually comes from poorly educated and impoverished adolescents who enter independence prematurely and are unable to perform their parental duties adequately. Their descendants do not inherit high quality genes and, in the absence of adequate care and education, may become the next generation of the poor or a hotbed for crime. Since killing violates the taboos of modern society, it would be better to prevent these defective groups from being born in the first place (as some studies have suggested, the US economy has benefited from the lower birth rate of potentially defective groups). However, the term "not born" here has a very ambiguous meaning. The malformed infant or the fetus aborted during pregnancy did *exist* once from the perspective of presence or absence; yet they are disposed of as the property of their parents, rather than being treated as independent individuals with their mouths shut, their fists tied, and their organs incompletely developed. Today, you might complain about your limited material enjoyment and your hard life full of frustrations due to your mediocre talent, but the single fact that you are alive proves that you were strong enough not to have been murdered in secret.

Today, we should also be vigilant of the phenomenon of social discrimination under the guise of evolutionary humanism, which is akin to Nazism in its essence. Social discrimination makes the same mistake as Nazism by attaching the label of inferiority to groups with certain characteristics, usually visible features: gender, sexual orientation, appearance, age (seniority system in workplace), race (racialism), ethnicity (caste system), etc. The correlation between inferior capability and these visible characteristics is non-existent (just as the white supremacy claimed by Nazism is nonsense), no matter how hard the perpetrators of discrimination try to persuade the public of the link between the two.

The rules of the game established by evolutionary humanism are regarded as fair because they stipulate that the assessment of one's competence is related solely to the outcome of social competition rather than any other intrinsic attributes, which are self-evident by definition. However, the perpetrators of discrimination can exclude victims with certain external characteristics from the competition from the outset once they manage to brainwash the public about their correlation to inferiority. They would then have a greater chance of winning, or even win outright, just because some of their visible characteristics are considered superior. This behavior is inherently a type of defamation; thus, it should be regulated by utilitarianism's reality principle and not be excused as the product of people's snide and hypocritical natures, through which those "degraded" characteristics will gradually become eliminated. It is discrimination itself that should be eliminated, rather than so-called "degraded" characteristics.

There are two strategies for coping with discrimination. The first is to change or disguise the attribute that is the subject of discrimination to cater to the masses; for example, homosexuals behave heteronormatively and homely people improve their appearance through plastic surgery. Though this brings immediate relief, it does not help to eliminate discrimination; in fact, those who are discriminated against would have surrendered to intolerance by taking such actions. The second strategy is to gather the power of vulnerable groups and fight against the perpetrators for the fundamental elimination of discrimination. Feminist movements and the fight for racial equality are examples of this strategy, which may encounter obstacles in the short term but comply with utilitarianism in the long term. "United we stand, divided we fall." Do not forget that the ghost of aggressive evolutionism is always waiting to act. If we, who could easily be reallocated to the defective group once the mutable rules change, do not learn how to join forces when facing discrimination, any one of us might be the next prey for its secret murder.

Social humanism (or communism) does not deny that one's ability is solely related to the results achieved under fair competition, but it regards "ability" as the same as other characteristics, such as "gender" and "appearance," which are insufficient to categorize humans and allocate resources accordingly. The intellect, as representative of one's overall abilities, is subject to intrinsic differences derived from one's genes in the same manner as other external representations and congenital characteristics. Is it not a new type of "discrimination by intellect" to distinguish the superior from the inferior based on a person's abilities? The social humanism of Mary Sue—an idealized and seemingly perfect fictional wish—affirms that all people are created equal, regardless of differences in gender, appearance… and ability. Social humanism eliminates both the pleasure experienced by winners and the pain experienced by losers in social competition by halting the game and distributing the rewards equally—the core concept of which holds that a social structure with an overall peaceful and average mentality is better than a social structure with some of the citizens feeling happy and the rest suffering pain.

However, the theory encounters difficulties in practice. Social members tend to be lazy at work under the premise of equal resource allocation. This lack of productivity could eventually drive the entire society to the edge of bankruptcy, since the enterprising spirit demonstrated by hard work is not derived from the calling of some noble morality but from sheer comparisons and self-interest. Without the goad of self-interest, everyone will do what serves their welfare best—that is, to contribute as little as possible, since one's share of social resources is always the same regardless of the amount of effort spent.

Today, social governance often combines the rules of social humanism with those of evolutionary humanism. We combat discrimination against certain external characteristics by social humanism through the rule that "all people are created equal." Simultaneously, we acknowledge the rules of evolutionary humanism by investing more resources in the competent and leaving the mediocre with less favorable choices. So, is such an admiration for "ability supremacy" fair and justified? Any behavior that complies with the will-to-live—that is, the desire for the human race to continue and prosper in the future—is regarded as fair and justified from the perspective of utilitarianism; therefore, there is no doubt about the fairness and justice of the supremacy of those with superior ability. Humans have ascended to the throne of hegemony on Earth not because of our beautiful appearance (we could not beat peacocks in a beauty contest), but because of our superior abilities (our greater intellect to be precise, since we cannot match lions or tigers in terms of physical strength). Therefore, it conforms to the interest/welfare of human evolution to continuously encourage improvements in ability through differential resource allocation. Moreover, although different individuals exhibit intrinsic differences in ability due to genetic inheritance, as is the case with other congenital characteristics such as gender and appearance, intellect is the most malleable quality. Intellect can be developed through hard work and an enabling environment, thus opening the widest scope of opportunities to everyone. Finally, today's society has recognized the diversity of human abilities, not just intellectual abilities, and provided platforms for geniuses with many different talents. Everyone can specialize in the development of their own inherited interests or strengths, and thereby help to achieve the diverse and complementary development of the entire human species.

Let us consider the conformity to utilitarianism by anti-utilitarian events after examining the violation of utilitarianism by seemingly utilitarian events. Reproduction is not the primary task for the parent in every situation, despite traditional beliefs. The reproductive function may even be abandoned as a sacrifice for the well-being of the parent under extreme conditions. For example, women of childbearing age would have undergone amenorrhea in the era of the Great Famine, when not even one drop of blood could afford to be wasted. "The drizzling amount of uterine bleeding during menstruation in fertile years is tantamount to excessive metrorrhagia in extreme conditions and it would be wise for the brain to close this hemorrhagic valve through endometrial atrophy" (Yi Xue Shou Zha, 2017, n.p.). The women's fertility could only be restored once sufficient food was available after they endured the famine or fled from the harsh environment; even when adults did not survive the famine, they could linger until their last breath without the burden of children. That being the case, why should adults not sacrifice themselves and entrust the survival and reproduction of the species to future generations? Because at birth there is no possibility of babies surviving without maternal care due to the unique fragility of human offspring. Human parents and their children are bound in such a symbiotic relationship that they stand or fall together; therefore, giving birth when the would-be parents can barely look after themselves is an action equivalent to suicide plus murder. This is the manifestation of utilitarianism in the crisis: the primary goal is the survival of the present population for as long as possible if there is no possibility of future reproduction. However, when humankind has the strength to persevere, the idea of giving up on one's own progress and entrusting one's hopes to future generations will reawaken. We find that lower classes, compared with middle and upper classes, tend to have stronger reproductive intentions and more children due to different reproductive costs. There are practical dilemmas behind such phenomena. For example, a country child with few siblings is very likely to be bullied by his/her peers, thus dragging every rural household into the vicious circle of excessive childbearing. However, the dominant reason lies in the fact that the parents have succumbed to their own misfortune and have entrusted the dream of ranking among the prestigious to future generations. It seems to them that the more children they have, the better their chance of overturning fate. The double standard of forcing children to progress while abandoning one's own progress is quite ironic. It is difficult to cultivate the children's potential with insufficient educational resources, resulting in an intergenerational transmission of poverty rather than an upward social mobility. It is not an effective strategy to seek to change the fate of the family by mass production without further attention. Human offspring, unlike the cubs of livestock that can stand and jump minutes after their birth, are extremely vulnerable at birth, which also accounts for the uncertainty and malleability of their future development. The cultivation of a child's innate potential is largely determined by the effort invested in his/her postnatal upbringing rather than any shortcuts.

The instinct to reproduce may be derived from the crisis awareness of one's own eventual mortality; thus, parents would always wish to leave behind the same number or even more individuals in future generations to take their place after their death. The mechanism of death and replacement is another indication of the utilitarian life-design of the will-to-live. The will-to-live deliberately sets a limit to the human lifespan through death to replace the aging and declining ancestors with new, burgeoning generations for the world and its limited resources, which indicates a very clear utilitarian judgement. It is more rewarding to render the limited resources to new generations than to older people, as the new generation's contribution to the evolutionary progress of the human race will far surpass that of older people. On the other hand, it also implies that we could have taken a different evolutionary path by extending the lifespan of each ancestor and slowing the replacement rate as much as possible to reduce the demand for new generations. In fact, the average human life expectancy is constantly increasing, with continuous improvements in health, technology, and nutrition. People in their fifties, who used to be called elders, are still in the workforce nowadays and far from retirement. Thus, it is not difficult to imagine that decrepit eighty-year-olds nowadays may qualify as middle-aged or even young in the future. The longevity of the existing population makes it less urgent to replace the death toll through reproduction, leading to a significant delay in the average age at which women marry and bear children.

It is reasonable for the will-to-live to limit the human lifespan to a short time over a long historical period. Older people become less able as they age and eventually fall behind the emerging young in all aspects. Moreover, the greatest significance of reproduction is to reshuffle the chromosomal arrangement that opens the neonatal mind to new knowledge and innovation. In contrast, older generations are prone to developing modes of thinking too rigid to adapt to environmental evolution. They may even resist social reforms to maintain society as it was in the "good old days," a society with which they are most comfortable until they become an obstacle to the progress of humankind and the evolution of society. The will-to-live always considers the overall welfare of the human species. It lifts the gavel for the final judgment: it is time to sentence them to death. Imagine what would happen if we prolonged the lifespan of *homo sapiens* in primitive society for no reason. All that early humans needed to learn was to distinguish fruits and vegetables and gather them, avoid predators, and hunt their prey so that they could survive in the wild; all this knowledge could be acquired in their first ten years of life. In the following years, they made their own living based on these skills and knowledge. Later, their deteriorating capabilities gradually made them a burden to the entire tribe. All they could do was lay idle and respect the young, who were not only physically stronger but also able to unshackle themselves from tradition, as they dared to experiment with new tools and techniques of hunting.

In most periods of history, the lifelong knowledge and skills required for work were very few, and one's life could be divided into the phases of learning, application, and recession. Once an individual enters the recession phase, he/she is of less value than young people who absorb knowledge rapidly and practice skills dexterously. The ancient concept that "Your life has a limit, but knowledge has none" (Zhuangzi cited in Kramer, 1986, p. 138) became more apt with the explosion of knowledge during the scientific revolution. Before that time, it was common for Europeans to respect the knowledgeable as "polymaths." Only after the explosion of knowledge did people realize that the amount of knowledge about the material world went far beyond the reach of any individual within a finite lifetime. Thereafter, people instituted the division of labor, with some specializing in research in this discipline and others focusing on learning of that subject. No one would aggrandize themselves as polymaths; at most, they were the experts in the little patch of their own field and hardly knew what to do outside their specialty.

The diverse development of all humankind mentioned previously can also be interpreted as the unilateral development of the single individual when we shift our perspective. When we encounter large, complicated tasks, we rely on the cooperation of different individuals today more than at any other time in history. It is true that the development of specialization and the division of labor has made social interactions as efficient as the assembly line, consequently increasing the overall capabilities of humankind. However, it fails to achieve comprehensive and independent individual development, as each person is reduced to a part of the giant social machine that cannot operate without the help of others. We are far less capable than our *homo sapiens* ancestors who had a good knowledge of the weather, animals, plants, tool making, etc., and who could survive independently in the wild.

The lack of comprehensive and independent individual development caused by the knowledge explosion has given us a reason to prolong life.

It is acceptable for us to succumb to being simply a part of the social machine, retiring at a certain stage and being replaced by a younger person with higher performance. Successors, with minds unshackled from any traditional presuppositions, often surprise their stubborn predecessors, who are trapped in an established consensus, with refreshing ideas, exemplifying the intergenerational upgrade in performance. Yet, such upgrades come at a cost. We must repeatedly provide a primary education for every batch of successors, just as we need to grind and polish newly made parts whenever we want to replace the old with the new. This repetitive investment in educational resources could be avoided by extending the enlistment time of current parts and further refining them based on existing performance. Imagine if we extend the lifespans of modern people, or to be precise, extend their phase of active learning and thinking; we, who once could master only a single field in our original limited lifetime, might be able to master more knowledge in multiple fields. Due to the cumulative effect of learning[13], those who are already accustomed to acquiring knowledge are more efficient in further study than those starting from scratch.

Thus, tasks that originally required the collaboration of multiple experts with one specialty each can be handled more efficiently by a single expert with multiple specialties through *cross-disciplinary thinking*—that is, to internalize external cooperation by combining knowledge of different fields within one's brain. Is such an evolutionary path not superior to an intergenerational upgrade in performance through the replacement of generations with assigned lifespans? In fact, greater longevity generates both a positive and a negative force on human evolution, under the interaction of which the human lifespan will eventually reach its optimal length instead of people becoming immortal in the traditional sense. On the one hand, life expectancy is prolonged → the phase of active learning and thinking is also extended → work that originally required cooperation among many people can now be completed by one person through cross-disciplinary thinking → improvement in work efficiency further develops human society → human life expectancy is extended further. On the other hand, life expectancy is prolonged → the post-learning and innovation phase is also extended → rigid thinking and dated ideas curb social development → a deteriorating human society in turn constrains life expectancy → humans replace the death toll by reproduction, which accelerates population re-

---

13 The cumulative effect of learning, also called the learning effect, is the process by which education increases productivity and facilitates further learning.

newal → the innovative new generation actively promotes social reforms → stagnant society progresses once again. Extending the lifespan of existing generations is a better evolutionary strategy than sexual propagation in the former scenario, and reproducing offspring is a better evolutionary strategy than the unrestrained longevity in the latter. Life expectancy will eventually reach an equilibrium between the interaction of the two.

You may already know about the complex manifestations of utilitarianism in different circumstances through previous reading. I will conclude this chapter by clarifying some common features and misunderstandings of utilitarianism. First, although this chapter vividly describes how the will-to-live imperceptibly influences and manipulates the behavior of human beings, there is in reality no such anthropomorphic character. The will-to-live does not employ loudspeakers to urge marriageable men and women to reproduce, nor does it calculate the residual value of adults and eliminate them before they become a burden to society. The so-called will-to-live is a simplified means of referring to the utilitarian calculations and tradeoffs in our conscious and sub-conscious minds and the variety of exquisite designs and physiological mechanisms in our bodies that serve the utilitarian purpose. Moreover, it does not entail that everyone consciously or unconsciously thinks in the way set out above; rather, it stands for the equilibrium outcome or mainstream view derived from the interactions and mutual restraints of people with all kinds of different thoughts.

Second, the judgment of utilitarianism is not based on consequentialism (the rightness or wrongness of any conduct is judged solely by its consequence). Nor is it founded upon the common misunderstanding of Hegelianism[14] ("what is rational is real and what is real is rational"), as if there were, behind all existing phenomena in reality, a rationale that conforms to utilitarianism and all existing phenomena should therefore be regarded as rational and justified. Unfortunately, many prevailing phenomena conflict with utilitarianism, such as social discrimination, whereas actions that spring from utilitarian intentions may eventually lead to undesirable results, such as the prisoner's dilemma[15] or the luxury trap. If we wish to establish whether a specific phenomenon complies with utilitarianism, we need to—in addition to reviewing its contemporary state of being—inves-

---

14 Hegelianism is the philosophy of G. W. F. Hegel. It can be summed up by the dictum that "the rational alone is real," which means that all reality is capable of being expressed in rational categories.

15 The prisoner's dilemma is a paradox in decision analysis in which two individuals acting in their own self-interests may result in a mutually dissatisfactory outcome.

tigate the incentives behind its emergence and its status in history as an equilibrium outcome or as an intermediate stage.

Further, the dialectic of utilitarianism lies in the fact that some behavior and strategies that are unprofitable in the short term are ultimately utilitarian with regard to their far-reaching benefits; other behavior or strategies that arise from a desire for quick success and instant benefits are anti-utilitarian in the long term—or, in the sense of higher tolerance, are merely trials and errors of an undeveloped prospect of utilitarianism. One famous example is the scientific theories designed to maximize utility developed under instrumentalism, as mentioned in the fourth chapter. Last, utilitarianism demonstrates the unity of opposites through the fact that most practices that deviate from mainstream values are utilitarian for the very reason of their scarcity. However, these practices often languish with no market price regardless of their intrinsic value, as they are largely ignored by the masses who are busy chasing hotspots in the mainstream—despite the diminishing marginal utility of those hotspots due to excessive supply. We should, therefore, always welcome the independent mind and seek beyond the simple pursuit of economic returns.

8

The Corralled "Free Will"

Core Question: Does Utilitarianism Overthrow Free Will?

You'lan Feng (2008) states in the book *Preface to Sansong Pavilion*:

> Pragmatism is characterized by its theory of truth, which is agnostic. It believes that human understanding comes from experience. What people can understand is limited to their experience. It is unknowable and meaningless to ask a question about what is beyond experience, because people can never develop an understanding outside the scope of their experience in any circumstances. Nevertheless, any attempt to solve such a question is also based on experience. So-called truth is nothing more than an explanation of experience that is also appropriate in complex circumstances. If it works, it is called Truth and regarded as useful to us. The true property of a theory is based on its usefulness, not on its so-called objectivity beyond the realm of experience. (p. 187)

The biggest problem of the utilitarian worldview is not agnosticism in my opinion, or further denying the existence of objective truth, but the lack of interest in exploring facts of little utilitarian value. The scientific practice that seeks to maximize utilitarian value is not necessarily more rewarding than one that is purely truth seeking; in the same manner, acts driven by utilitarianism may not necessarily yield outcomes in conformity with utilitarianism, a fact that reflects the complexity and the dialectic of the theory.

In contrast, utilitarianism is tremendously passionate about the part of the world whose study unearths significant value. Since there is nothing more significant from a human perspective than facts relevant to ourselves, we are very worried about whether our free will really exists or whether all our actions are based on utilitarian considerations and can be eventually reduced to complex manifestations of the simple principle "gaining advantage and avoiding harm" in different situations. My answer is that free will might well exist, but it depends on how we define "free will." Suppose there is a group of deer in the forest. They will certainly flee when they notice an approaching predator, and we can identify the clear causal relationship between the cause and its effect—the deer escape the situation. When deer are grazing casually in the forest, however, some of them might look to the right in vigilance; while others may look to the left to seduce potential mates or simply out of idleness. In any case, there are always specific reasons for the different directions of each deer's glance, which are difficult to determine as we can neither speak the language of the deer nor read their minds. Moreover, we have absolutely no interest in identifying what are likely to be frivolous reasons, so we casually conclude that it is a random and contingent behavior for a deer to look to the right or the left without ascribing the behavior to the free will of each deer. The conclusion would be very different if we replaced the deer in the scenario with people. In certain situations, a crowd will demonstrate a consistent behavioral pattern of gaining advantage and avoiding harm, and the decisive role of utilitarianism in guiding human practice seems irrefutable. In other situations, however, individuals in the crowd behave randomly and contingently, just as the deer did, yet we praise such random acts as being guided by the free will of each individual at this time.

As demonstrated by these examples, free will does not refute the causal relationship. There is no doubt that everyone has their own considerations, motives, and even plans behind their behavior. What free will has exposed is our limited ability to speculate on the causes of behavior and our failure to predict future human behavior even if we have derived some common laws of behavior (such as utilitarianism) from the various actions of the crowd. However, it is of extraordinary significance for humans to identify the cause of each person's behavior and predict future trends on that basis, so we have created the concept of "free will" to conceal our predicament when we fail to do so. Meanwhile, it is also unconventional for us to dig into the reasons behind behavior of little utilitarian value. We tend to attribute it casually, and mistakenly, to some kind of contingent representation without causation. As a result, people often misunderstand that free will is as much against the determinism/causal relationship as is behavior of little utilitarian value.

As written in Part One-Truth, whether different occurrences obey a causal relationship is one thing; whether we can apply these causal relationships to accurately predict the future is entirely another. The limitations in applications, such as predicting future events, do not overturn the objective reality of determinism and causation. In fact, this is the key to understanding human free will and even the Uncertainty Principle in the subatomic dimension. Our recognition that human beings have free will or that the position and momentum (velocity) of one electron cannot be precisely measured at the same time does not entail there being no causal relationship determining human behavior or electronic movement. Rather, these causalities provide insufficient information for us to predict future human behavior or the future movement of electrons. It is precisely because of the limited practical value of the causal relationship that we would save ourselves effort in seeking to uncover the mystery inside the "black box" and compromise with vague and generalized words such as "free" and "uncertain" in our description of its internal principles. (Meanwhile, we also currently lack the capacity to document the causal chain.)

It is difficult to predict future trends in disciplines with not only Second Order Chaos[16] but also First Order Chaos,[17] even after explicating their internal casual relationships. It is arrogant for humans to believe that we are capable of making accurate predictions of physical phenomena once we have comprehended the physical mechanisms that drive them. Take weather forecasts as an example: we can predict the weather with great precision only a few hours in advance, even with a full comprehension of atmospheric conditions. The more distant the future, the less accurate our forecast. Another example is Schrodinger's Cat: if we put a cat and a small amount of radioactive material into a box, there is a fifty percent chance that the radioactive material will decay and release toxic gas that will kill the cat and a fifty percent chance that the radioactive material will not decay and the cat will survive. When the box is closed, the entire system

---

16   Second Order Chaos means that the prediction made for a process itself will affect the evolution of the process.

17   First Order Chaos means that the prediction made for a process itself will not affect the evolution of the process.

maintains a wave state of uncertainty—that is, a superimposition of the cat being both dead and alive. Whether the cat is dead or alive can only be determined after the box is opened and observed by external parties. However, we can be certain that the cat died without opening the box if we wait long enough. Either the material will decay once the elapsed time exceeds its half-life (assuming it is a short-lived radioactive material) or the cat will die from its own limited lifespan even if it is not poisoned by the radioactive material. Finally, let us return to Heisenberg's Uncertainty Principle. Can we not make any clear assertions about the movement of electrons, even though the position and the momentum (velocity) of one electron cannot be precisely measured at the same time? Of course we can! At the very least, we can assert that the electrons must circulate the nucleus, no matter how uncertain their specific movement patterns might be.

The examples set out above demonstrate that our predictions often lack value due to limited foresight or excessive time lags (e.g., the weather forecast), even if we have explicated some principles of the phenomena. We are still able to draw some convergent (e.g., the cat's ultimate fate of death) or generalized (e.g., the orbit of electrons around the nucleus) conclusions about the phenomena, although we cannot explain their internal mechanisms, which lack values as well. Therefore, mastering the principles has little significance in guiding practice at the same time-space scale.

How would things change when they scale from the microscopic to the macroscopic? The contingent representation of electronic movement is always confined within a limited range—the orbit around the nucleus—no matter how unpredictable the detailed movement of each electron; thus, this unpredictability does not influence the overall structure and chemical property of the atom (except for certain radioactive elements). The contingency of electronic movement does not tamper with the chemical reactions or the principles underlying the interactions between atoms and molecules based on the unit of the atom, not to mention the biological reactions and principles of the interactions between chemicals and organic compounds based on the unit of the molecule. Relative to quantum mechanics, the focus of chemistry and biology research is at the macro level. Causal relationships at the macroscopic scale hold independently, regardless of uncertainty at the microscopic scale.

In fact, the two paragraphs above provide possibilities for the following hypotheses: uncertainty about micro-scale principles will *not* create major inadequacies in the interpretation of either macro or micro phenomena, as the principles have little value in predicting phenomena at the same micro scale, and their range of influence is too limited to disrupt phenomena at the macro scale. On the contrary, it might be more *useful* to allow room for such uncertainty in the principles than to introduce some pseudo-causation when explaining external phenomena. But how is this possible in the real world? Suppose you have received a request from a pharmaceutical manufacturer to forecast the revenue (R) of a new drug that is going to launch on the market at price (P) for the first 10 years. After inspecting the demand (D) for the drug and its growth trend over the 10 years, you can calculate the revenue by multiplying the price by the demand for each year. With some industry knowledge, you may introduce another parameter—the probability of success (S)—to the equation (4.1), since the government may prohibit a drug from entry into the market if its benefit does not compensate for its cost from the pharmacoeconomic perspective.

$$R = SPD \tag{4.1}$$

Instead of wrecking the deal completely, the government may bargain for a cheaper drug price in exchange for its access to the market. Depending on the negotiation power of the government and the manufacturer, there could be multiple price points ($P_1, P_2, P_3..., 0 < P_n < P$) that both sides may potentially agree on, each of which has a different probability of success.

$$R = \bar{P}D \quad \bar{P} = P_1 S_1 + P_2 S_2 + \cdots + P_n S_n \tag{4.2}$$

$$\begin{cases} R_1 = P_1 D_1 \\ R_2 = P_2 D_2 \\ \quad \cdots \\ R_n = P_n D_n \end{cases} \tag{4.3}$$

A sophisticated consultant would present parallel scenarios of revenue when the drug is priced at different values (4.3), instead of a singular revenue extrapolated from the weight-averaged price (4.2). This strategy features multiple advantages. First, the market demand is correlated with the price level; the higher the price, the fewer the patients who can afford the drug, and the lower the demand. Pairing a specific D_n with a specific P_n better describes the market size of a certain scenario than does a constant D for all price levels. Moreover, the drug will be labeled with a finite price once released—either at $P_1, P_2...$ or 0 in the worst scenario. It will surely not be priced at $\bar{P}$, which is merely a weighted average of all possibilities. Once the uncertain drug price collapses to a finite value assumed by one equation of the presented parallel scenarios, that "lucky" equation could simulate the market performance of the new drug for the first 10 years much better than one single weight-averaged equation that "seems" to take every possibility into consideration. The only drawback to this approach is that it consumes more processing and storage than does the conventional approach of using the weighted-average method. While the latter just generates a series of chronological revenue numbers, the former may require one to run a program to exploit all revenue potentials proposed by the parallel scenarios, because before market entry, any price is possible. Sound familiar? As some quantum physicists put it, "without perception, everything exists." This is also likely to be the reason why quantum mechanics, with its algorithms based on the Uncertainty Principle, is so successful.

However, "true wisdom is to know what you do not know" (Confucius, 2015, p 13). We can either admit with candidness that we lack the capability at present to explicate the operating mechanism of microscopic objects without interfering with the object itself. Alternatively, we can arrogantly claim that it is not necessary for us to expend tremendous effort to explore the mechanism further, given the success of uncertainty in quantum mechanics; understanding how the electrons work will not have a great impact on the study of chemistry and biology. However, we cannot deny the objective reality of the causal relationship at the micro scale, nor can we further assert that there are no grounds for causation and determinism apart from probabilistic events at the macro scale based on the questionable premise that there is no certainty, only contingency, at the micro scale. The current predicament of quantum mechanics is similar to those of disciplines that are subject to Second Order Chaos, such as economics. That is to say, the prediction made for a process itself will affect the evolution of the process. The best way to verify any particular economic theory is therefore to keep it secret until the market reaction complies with the theoretical prediction. However, the masses are likely to treat the belated announcement as being wise after the event. Research into electronic movement is much simpler by comparison. The electron won't change its trajectory based on human theories, unlike *homo economicus*, but it will change its trajectory due to the interference of the observation. Therefore, all we need to do is to—in a manner of speaking—track a suspect without being discovered.

Free will is similar to the Uncertainty Principle at the quantum level in that it describes the uncertainty of individual behavior at the micro economic and social levels. It is also confined to the limited range of maximizing utilitarian values, that is, behaving in accordance with utilitarianism. In other words, free will is like a flock of sheep that is herded inside the fence of utilitarianism where only limited activities are allowed. The uncertainty of individual behavior caused by free will may create difficulties in the study of individual psychology and microeconomics, but it will not affect the study of history and sociology, where the unit of observation is the group, crowd, community, or society, since the causal relationships in macroscopic studies hold outside the influential range of microscopic uncertainty. Hence, such microscopic uncertainty can be subsumed under the general name of utilitarianism. Imagine that one day we have invented a mind-reading device capable of identifying the psychological determinants, rather than so-called "free will," behind the random behavior of a person; would we be able to predict all their future behavior accurately? Like the weather forecast, we would be able to make the most accurate predictions about behavior seconds after reading a person's mind, but our predictions would become less certain as the future recedes. The reason for this increasing uncertainty lies in the fact that mental activity at a particular moment determines mental activity at the next moment, which further determines mental activity at a moment after... Accordingly, can we not always specify a particular state of mental activity and the behavior it determines no matter how distant the future? No, because an individual's mentality is influenced not only by the person's history but also by his/her external environment, which is likely to differ more and more from the initial conditions over time. Moreover, environmental changes cannot be read or predicted by the mind-reading device. We do not even know where to begin the invention of a special environmental device to monitor the aspects of the environment prone to change. There are too many uncontrollable variables to monitor, which fundamentally exposes our limited ability to exhaust and digest all information. The explicated causal relationship still has limitations as practice guidance even after unveiling the mask of free will, just like the Internet meme, "Heard many words about life, but still living a hard time."

I mentioned at the beginning of this section that free will might well exist, but it depends on how we define the term. The mind-reading device or technique that uncovers the psychological determinants behind seemingly random behavior will be invented at some point in our long technological trajectory. Therefore, free will should not be defined as, "There is no causal relationship that determines individual behavior; therefore, the individual can behave at will." If we want the concept of free will to endure, it should instead be defined as, "There is still the room and possibility for future individual behavior to deviate from theoretical predictions, even after explicating the decisive causal relationships behind current behavior." Note that this statement does not hold in reverse. Once a certain future behavior occurs, we can definitely trace it to its source and identify the historical reason that generated the behavior. The role of free will can at best be ascribed to the inaccurate predictions of the future, not the incomplete explanations of the history. By the same token, once we have managed to simultaneously measure an electron's position and momentum without interfering with the microscopic object itself, the Uncertainty Principle at the subatomic level should be redefined as the Unpredictability Principle. There is still room for future electronic movement to deviate from theoretical predictions, even after simultaneously determining the current position and momentum of the electron, e.g., due to the co-existing trajectories of multiple forms.

9

Sunday Mass Unattended by God

*Core Question: Will the Human Species Evolve
into Superman or even into God?*

Plato records Socrates saying at his trial, "An unexamined life is not worth living" (cited in Adler, 1997, p. 77). We cannot avoid a discussion about how to lead one's life before the end of the part on ethics (despite "heard many words about life, but still living a hard time"). The next chapter of this part will elaborate on how individuals should make choices when their personal pursuits systematically and irreconcilably collide with the expectations of the social mainstream. To do this, we first explore a range of outlooks on life from a macro perspective; that is, what kind of life can be logically justified as the perfect life under the guidance of utilitarianism? And what kind of life is worth pursuing?

Unlike the happy life, which may differ from person to person depending on their subjective sensibilities and diversified interests, there must be an objective standard in society for the perfect life, as it involves a value judgment. The perfect life as a philosophical concept is immeasurably expansive, similar to the metaphor of the brain in a vat (Harman, 1973). The metaphor imagines the immersion of a human brain into a vat filled with a solution of not only happiness-inducing chemicals, such as dopamine and endorphin, but also other substances that help to fabricate the illusion of reality. In fact, the perfect life must contain the complete range of emotional experiences, including joy, trust, fear, surprise, sadness, anticipation, anger, and disgust, because the concept of completion is, by definition, within the scope of perfection. The superiority of the perfect life lies in the fact that it spares us from actual failure and frustration while granting us the emotions of sadness, anger, and disgust; it spares us from actual failure and frustration while imparting to us the skills, knowledge, and insights that can be obtained only through failure and frustration. As it is not the specific negative experience itself but the insight and reflection gained from such an experience that is of benefit, undergoing the negative event itself becomes meaningless in our scenario[18]—and there is no room for meaninglessness in the perfect life. Likewise, the perfect life can also spare us from actual positive experiences while granting us the emotions of joy, surprise, and anticipation. The essence of all experience is nothing more than its use as a tool for obtaining insight. A perfect life would omit the meaningless experiences and go straight to the harvest of meaningful insights, since gaining insight through an occurrence is extremely inefficient and does not differ from the acquired learning processes of an ordinary life; again, the concept of inefficiency is excluded from the scope of perfection. A perfect life grants us epiphanies because of its high efficiency.

In conclusion, what would the perfect life be like if it really existed in the world? It is probably the most beautiful firework that exploded in a flash and the disillusion that never ceased after its bloom; for one to apprehend everything in the world at the instant of birth would be to achieve a God-like state of omniscience and omnipotence—only for him/her to turn around and embrace death without hesitation. Why is that? Why would one choose to end his/her life after reaching the near-divine state of omniscience and omnipotence? Because achieving perfection means that there is no room for further improvement; instead, any further experience after perfection merely adds to the blasphemy and waste of such perfection. Why should we bear these meaningless happenings when there is no stage superior to the status quo—the ultimate perfection? It is no surprise that one would reduce such blasphemy and waste to the minimum; it is no surprise that one would seal the ultimate beauty of the moment in the vast void. One step to perfection; the next, to annihilation. Once the development of something reaches the ultimate goal of perfection, nothing further is possible.

The words of Silenus, "What is best of all is utterly beyond your reach: not to be born, not to be, to be nothing. But the second-best thing for you—

---

18 Si'da Jiang raised this point in a debate on the talk show *U can U BiBi*: if there is a button that can customize the perfect life for your child, would you as a parent press the button? (16th episode of Season 4).

is to die soon," (Nietzshe, 1997a, p.21) represent a strongly pessimistic outlook on life. The journey of life is a continuous accumulation of negatives, and no positive value is possible. The most highly recommended behavior is to stop losses as early as possible—the so-called, "to die soon"—to retain the total value of life at close to zero. Today, we surpass such pessimism. We grow more ambitious in our pursuit of perfection. We believe that the near-divine state of omniscience and omnipotence is reachable. The key lies in "what next?" Perfection happens when our life reaches its peak, and every second after summiting depreciates its value. By the time all roads lead to Rome, embracing death may demonstrate the greatest respect possible for the instant of ultimate perfection.

Someone may question if there can be a more positive attitude to life after one has lived a perfect life in the near-divine state of omniscience and omnipotence. For example, to live not for selfish gain but for the improvement of social welfare through using one's accumulated knowledge and power. There is a Japanese anime named *Psycho-Pass* that describes an absurd hypothetical world wherein a futuristic society is governed by the Sibyl System, a powerful network of psychometric scanners built up by a collection of brains in vats. The Sibyl System surveils daily life and establishes moral and behavioral codes for community members. The psychological health of every citizen is monitored in real time by the Sibyl System. Those with sub-standard mental health are forced to receive psychotherapy; to nip potential crime in the bud, those whose mental states have deteriorated to warning levels are detained as potential criminals before they actually commit any atrocities. The donors of the brains in the vats that make up the Sibyl System used to be talented people in different areas who were willing to become the top decision makers by donating their brains and sacrificing their own flesh in the process. However, in some aspects, they didn't lose their bodies. Commanding the police, manipulating politics, and interfering with diplomacy...These have all become their new and more powerful limbs and muscles, with which they have surpassed other monitored citizens and reached the status of the prophet Sibyl. Nevertheless, the system could only prevent evil by first understanding evil. Therefore, the Sibyl System does not incorporate only the brains of talented people but also the brains, and consequently the memories, of captured criminal geniuses to develop a thorough comprehension of the criminal mind without actually committing the crimes. Later, the system discovers that no matter how intently it studies the criminal mind, there are always higher-order criminal geniuses who can openly commit crimes with apparently healthy mentalities under surveillance. They are immune to psychometrics. Finally, the Sibyl System encounters the ultimate conundrum: if each individual in the group takes a seemingly inconsequential action unconsciously, rather than with evil intent, and these actions later aggregate into a powerful crime, should the mass incidence of unconscious evil be sanctioned? How could the system foretell such evil and segregate each individual from the group in advance?

Therefore, if an omniscient and omnipotent God does exist, He/She may have already understood that wickedness is to goodness as shadow is to light. The brighter the light of goodness, the darker the shadow of wickedness, since the two evolved at the same time. It would be vain to try to create an all-illuminated world with the power of God. Helping the shoots grow by pulling them upward[19] would only disturb the natural evolutionary process and create problems that are too difficult to be solved by humankind at a premature stage. Thus, "not-doing" is left as the optimal choice, and there is no need to linger over the world.

In addition, we need to unpack the definitions of omniscience and omnipotence. First, omnipotence does not necessarily mean "must do," it can also mean choosing to do nothing ("not-doing," or non-action). One malicious and ineffective claim raised by atheists to prove that God does not exist is that God would certainly not mind digging through feces, since He is omnipotent. How could devout Christians refute this offensive claim without diminishing the all-encompassing power of the God in whom they believe? Well, the ability to dig through feces is not unusual, as anyone can do it. God's superiority lies in the fact that He can know the taste of feces without actually digging through them, while an ordinary mortal has no other option but to find out firsthand. The fact that God *can* dig through feces does not mean that God *will* dig through feces. Second, the scope of omnipotence is restrained by omniscience. Omniscience is the knowledge of everything, including all the laws in the objective world, thus knowing what one can and what one cannot do—God is capable of anything in compliance with natural laws and incapable of anything that violates natural laws. One might argue that this assertion is based on the premise that natural laws cannot be altered. If God is truly omnipotent, He should be able to change natural laws effortlessly and reveal Himself though signs or miracles against common knowledge, not just through the usual phenomena in compliance with natural laws. Does God still need to be "scient" (knowledgeable), not to mention "omniscient," if natural laws can be

---

19   A Chinese idiomatic saying to convey that things are usually spoiled when one tries to be too helpful.

altered wantonly? God wouldn't take any notice of natural laws in the first place and just act as presumptuously as an ignorant child if natural laws no longer stood under His power. We have assumed that God's so-called omnipotence denotes all possible actions under the rule of objective laws once we have placed omniscience before omnipotence.

Finally, is God good all the time? "Goodness" here is judged from the perspective of humans.

> The fundamental insight of polytheism, which distinguishes it from monotheism, is that the supreme power governing the world is devoid of interests and biases and is therefore unconcerned with the mundane desires, cares, and worries of humans. It is pointless to ask this power for victory in war, for health, or for rain, which is quite similar to the natural laws of today. On the other hand, polytheists also believe in many partial and biased powers under this supreme power. It was not until monotheism that people attached the quality of goodness to the only God, believing that the supreme power of the universe is dedicated to humanity (Harari, 2017, pp. 203-206).

So is God good when He reaches Nirvana[20] at the instant of His birth (as described in the perfect life above)? God regards it as the optimal choice to pass away by doing nothing from His all-encompassing vantage point, after foretelling all future consequences and evaluating all trade-offs caused by the abuse of power. Yet, mundane disciples eager for the fulfillment of their own desires through the hand of the Lord may not be able to appreciate the kindness of "not-doing" demonstrated by God. They would have turned to supermen for help, whose dedication to mankind would outweigh their inferior powers, had they known that God with His completely transcendent mind would not bring them any utilitarian benefit.

Today, we are attracted to the states of omniscience and omnipotence in the perfect life on one hand, while on the other we want to avoid the transcendent and pessimistic outlook on life that accompanies this perfect state. There is no need to worry about such a mentality, however, since the ultimate goal of projects aiming to extend life, such as genome editing

---

20   A transcendent state in Buddhism where the subject is released from the cycle of death and rebirth, similar to the words of Silenus—not to be born, not to be, to be nothing.

or Project Gilgamesh,[21] is to create neo-humans with greater knowledge and capabilities to better serve society, rather than to create a God who is devoid of interests and considers "not-doing" to be the ultimate goodness. In the objective sense, no matter how much neo-humans evolve in knowledge and capability, they will be able to get infinitely close to but never reach the divine state of omniscience and omnipotence. As long as there is still a gap between them and perfection, there is still room for improvement and more utilitarian guidance for action than "not-doing." When we discuss the perfect life, what are we talking about? We are talking about our attitude toward perfection, which is worth pursuing but can never be regarded as achieved. Our lives have been improving all the time. If one day our lives become satisfactory enough, we should raise the standard of perfection rather than admit we have reached the perfect state. Don't stop the pace of progress and don't look for shortcuts for fear of hard work on the painstaking journey to perfection. Perfection is like the hanging moon in the sky that illuminates our road ahead. Enjoy the moonlight along the way. Arrival is never the goal.

It is of great significance for one to pursue improvements in knowledge and capability during one's single life in modern society, where the individual is treated as a part of the giant social machine and his/her development is limited to achieving the function of the part. In terms of how to lead one's life, Arthur Schopenhauer once warned:

> Scholars are those who have read in books, but thinkers, men of genius, world-enlighteners, and reformers of the human race are those who have read directly in the book of the world. At bottom, only our fundamental ideas have truth and life; for it is they alone [that] we really and thoroughly understand. The ideas of someone else which we have read are scraps and leavings of someone else's meal, the cast-off clothes of a stranger (Schopenhauer, 1851/1974, p. 492).

As civilization continues to develop, we increasingly depend on the ideas of our predecessors and hope to make further refinements of their ideas rather than explore the first and second tier world as independent pioneers. The truly wise often flee from the places where the masses desperately try to integrate. He/She strolls alone in the wilderness isolated

---

[21] A human reconstruction program that aims to dramatically increase bodily functions, prevent and treat difficult diseases that threaten human health, and substantially extend human life.

from human civilization by blazing a new trail through brambles; at the end of the road, should his/her heart rest in peace on a Sunday unattended by God.

Renyuan Dong

EPILOGUE 2
To the Masses As Well As to the Mavericks

Core Question: Systematic Value Conflicts—How to Deal with the Conflict between Pursuit for Self and Social Demands?

Kahlil Gibran (2001) has written a parable on this topic entitled *The Wise King*:

> Once there ruled in the distant city of Wirani a king who was both mighty and wise. And he was feared for his might and loved for his wisdom. Now, in the heart of that city was a well, whose water was cool and crystalline, from which all the inhabitants drank, even the king and his courtiers, for there was no other well.
>
> One night when all were asleep, a witch entered the city, and poured seven drops of strange liquid into the well, and said, "From this hour whoever drinks this water shall become mad."
>
> Next morning all the inhabitants save the king and his lord chamberlain, drank from the well and became mad, even as the witch had foretold. And during that day, the people in the narrow streets and in the market places did naught but whisper to one another, "The king is mad. Our king and his lord

chamberlain have lost their reason. Surely, we cannot be ruled by a mad king. We must dethrone him."

That evening the king ordered a golden goblet to be filled from the well. And when it was brought to him, he drank deeply, and gave it to his lord chamberlain to drink.

And there was great rejoicing in that distant city of Wirani, because its king and its lord chamberlain had regained their reason (p. 27).

We can easily rewrite this parable into a completely different version from another perspective.

> We were a group of reticent, introverted, and wise children who loved to meditate and watch the stars. My companions in the kindergarten were all like this as far as I knew, so I supposed the rest of the world to be the same, even without going outside.
>
> We could read each other's thoughts through eye contact. Hence, we enjoyed exploring our internal worlds more than interfering with others. We had a beautiful name, "Children of the Stars." We believed that the world should be as quiet and peaceful as we were.
>
> But one day, for unknown reasons, the companions around me began to go insane. They kept lingering while wagging their heads and limbs tirelessly; they became a verbose crowd, harping on trivial matters all the time…
>
> Gradually did I notice that they had been deceived by a witch who disguised herself as the new doorkeeper of the kindergarten, and they had drunk the water she had prepared that would make people go mad.
>
> Eventually, the witch approached me. She wore a white robe and carried a glass of water in her hand, trying to harm me. I protested mutely with my mouth firmly shut to demonstrate my resolution not to drink the water.
>
> She had a hectic smile on her face and said, "You are the last autistic child in the world. Come and take the medicine. Let me save you from loneliness and self-closure."

Today, we still don't have any effective cure for autism. If an effective drug is invented for the treatment of autistic people one day, I'm afraid the story above will be the true voice of the hearts of those autistic children who are forced to take the medication. How could we tell whether the water from the well is the poison to make people go mad or the antidote to wake someone up to the world as a wiser person? Moreover, how could we as medical workers arrogantly assert that the world of people with autism is inferior to that of ordinary people, and thereby feed them drugs out of self-righteousness to "save" them from loneliness without respecting their own will? People always esteem and praise the cultural environment and value system that they are familiar with and tend to denigrate and vilify foreign cultures and values without exception. Every maverick upholding his/her own unique values and the masses accepting mainstream social values would both consider the other side to be mad. In that case, is there an objective measure to judge who is right and who is wrong; which set of values is superior and which is inferior?

We would often make ridiculous and inconsistent judgments if we stand on one side and try to observe and evaluate the world on the other side with a so-called "tolerant and open" mind. Let us return to the example of the water in the well that deranges people. If you noticed that all the other people in the world who had drunk the well water were idling away their time in all kinds of pleasure seeking rather than the duty of reproduction, you would develop an awareness of the looming crisis of human extinction. At the time you would not only refuse to drink the water, but would also very likely kidnap a fool of the opposite sex and force them to have sex with you regardless of your gender, sexual orientation, aspiration to bachelordom or DINK lifestyle, etc. "Is this rape?" you asked yourself. "No, I am just ensuring the continuation of the human race. What an honorable mission that is!" However, you hadn't fled the fools' world with your newborn baby before you discovered that citizens didn't reproduce because there was no longer a need for it. The well water you thought deranged people actually made them immortal. There was no need to supplement the population with new people, since the present population did not deteriorate. You would booze the well water as soon as you realized that humans' long-cherished wish for immortality was achieved with a sip of the holy water. Before you could enjoy eternal life after imbibing to your heart's content, once again came news: the citizens had become cannibals. They killed and ate one other, which was also quite understandable. On this side of the world (the rational world), humans are born with a limited lifespan and evolve through the production of new generations. On the other side of the world (the fools' world), however, the human body is eternal, and the fools believe (which may also be true) that the only way to evolve in knowledge and skills is to eat other people. When one eats another, the cannibal will acquire all the memories, knowledge, and skills of the eaten. The more people one eats, the more capabilities from different individuals are aggregated into one person and transform him/her into a stronger creature. If you were left with a trace of reason on this side of the world, you would more than regret having drunk up the water, and even wish to throw it up, but it would be too late. You would happily join the feast of human cannibalism in the fools' world at that time.

As you can see, the operating rules of these two worlds can be implemented independently without coming into conflict, yet it would result in a peculiar play of absurdist fiction if we tried to proceed from the rules of one side to the other or to merge the two sets of rules into one.

Let us return to the question of whether there is an objective measure by which to judge the superiority of different values, given the epistemological dilemma that the subject of a world can never justify his/her cognition of the world from God's perspective (the objective perspective of a third party) because he/she is always captive to his/her own subjective perspective. We cannot make objective and unbiased assessments of different cultures and values when we are inevitably involved as interested parties, unlike God, who looks on mundane matters as a disinterested bystander. Instead, we tend to maintain the existing cultural environment if we benefit from it and actively introduce new cultures if we are struggling in the current one. Therefore, evaluating another unknown and unexperienced world from our subjective perspective is all we are capable of, despite its unreliability. We have to admit with resignation that if we perceive another world as a fool's country from our subjective perspective, there is a significant possibility that it is indeed an undesirable world in the objective sense.

The short manga *Vampire* by Fujiko Fujio[22] tells us that we can only develop a true understanding of a different world by experiencing it directly and overthrowing our established mindset from the familiar world. The hero and heroine in the manga were afraid to become vampires at first because the moon is perceived as red in the eyes of vampires. It was not until they became vampires that they discovered the beauty of the red

---

22   The topic of the talk show *U can U BiBi* in the semi-final of season 4 is: Should you, as the last rational person in the world, drink the well water that deranges people when everyone else has already drunk it and gone mad? The guest Ru'jin Yan mentioned *Vampire* by Fujiko Fujio.

moon. What the manga *Vampire* doesn't tell us is that once the protagonists regard the red moon as beautiful, they must recall the bright moonlight appreciated at the time when they were still humans as gloomy: a pale nightmare that haunts their sleep. Taking the poisonous/holy water does not make you embrace a new world while retaining the complete memory or justified evaluation of a previous world dramatically different from it to further enrich your life by building an open and tolerant mind. Instead, it introduces you to a new world that might be either good or bad and needs to be verified by your own experience; as the price, it must make you abandon, forget, or feel disgust for your previous world, which is also either good or bad but is already well known to you.

In fact, every one of us will drink the water of forgetfulness one day. If you believe in the theory of reincarnation, you know that our shades after death are required to drink the water of Lethe, the river of forgetfulness, to completely erase the memory of our past life. Then we are reincarnated as another person, with different default settings in nationality, gender, family, and other background factors, and we step into a new world, growing a neoteric outlook on life and values. The experiences in our past life, due to complete forgetfulness, will not enrich our new life or help us to build more open and tolerant minds to embrace change and diversity. Now, before the advent of reincarnation, why should you end your present life by drinking the poisonous/holy water by yourselves? In the absence of objective measures to judge the superiority of different values, why should you adjust to mainstream social values and give up your personal pursuits? The only reason to do so may lie in the unparalleled power of the two sets of values, which make the individual bow to group pressure. The only courage to insist on yourself and withstand group pressure comes from the answer to the question, "How much do you love yourself?"

To drink the poisonous/holy water, or not to drink? To join the group dance in the new world, or to defend the lost city of Atlantis alone? As I wrote in Chapter 7, utilitarianism demonstrates the unity of opposites through the fact that most practices that deviate from mainstream values are utilitarian for the very reason of their scarcity. The value of preserving those maverick, marginal, or limbo worlds for the mainstream world is that, if a plague erupts in the mainstream world, the citizens would flee to the deserted city gate of the former for refuge. The marginal or limbo worlds that have long been forgotten would serve as their last shelter, just as Marxism, with its emphasis on government intervention, usually lacks attention in the West but undergoes a resurgence every time there is an economic crisis in the free market.

But what if there is no plague in the mainstream world? Are you willing to be the grave-keeper of the lost civilization all through your life? One question would strike you to your heart: How much do you love yourself? Enough to be willing to safeguard your inner world, overlooked by the mainstream, at any price? If you live in a world with hustle and bustle and I ask you on the street, "Do you love this world?" it will be hard for you to answer in front of others; hence, your answer is too inconsequential to determine the fate of the world. If you live in a world left by everyone except you and once again, I ask, "Do you love this world?" the question is equivalent to, "Do you love yourself?" The whole world is left with and represented by its only resident—you. If you do, then you stay as the last fruit of this civilization; if you do not, then you leave for a new world where you may fall in love with yourself again.

It is difficult to be alone when the crowds are bustling around, but you have a valuable opportunity, without any time limit, to make a conversation with yourself when the world is left with only you. The saints teach us to be self-restrained when one is all alone, but I would say that you might as well be honest and candid, releasing the dark side of your heart, facing the self-abasement you try to hide, and listing the injuries you've suffered from confrontation with the mainstream to protect your own world. I know this is difficult because humans are good at self-delusion and self-reconciliation. This time, however, you don't need to pretend to be strong any more, as there are no longer eyes peering and mouths snickering when you lick the wounds. Why bother admitting that you are a complete loser in this world? This world is about to end anyway, but you can set sail again in another new world. Only if the answer to the question above (do you love yourself?), after undergoing such self-exposure to one's failures and drawbacks, remains positive is such self-love beyond the frivolous scope of narcissism and strong enough to guide you through the endless night of the lonely life.

A Thai movie entitled *Fathers* realistically depicts many educational difficulties faced by a homosexual couple after they adopt a child in a society where same-sex marriage is legal. One scene impressed me: when the gay couple discovered the child imitated adult behavior and showed extra intimacy to the same sex, they were afraid that their child would grow up gay like them. A representative from a children's aid organization visited them with the information that the natural mother of the child had been found and tried to persuade the couple to return the child to the mother for a while, saying, "If you had a choice, you would not wish your child to be gay as well!" The tacit assent of the couple shocked me, as they were homosexuals themselves. Even though they ranked among the upper class of the society in the movie and enjoyed the same rights in marriage and adoption as heterosexual couples, they still could not get rid of the self-abasement often seen among sexual minorities. Equal rights will not be truly achieved until the day when both homosexual and heterosexual parents can say with pride, "I do not mind if my children are gay or straight. I respect their own choices," rather than, "I do not discriminate against homosexuals, but I do not want my child to be one."

Of course, you may feel abased today for more common reasons, such as an inferior intellect or other limited capabilities. By the time this sober world is left with only you, you look around the empty kingdom and realize you have already become the smartest person, given that the others have gone mad. You are surprised that this does not make you any happier. What has long shamed you is not inferiority of intellect or other capabilities, but the discrimination and unequal treatment that have hindered you from fitting into the group, as well as your cowardice in not fighting back. You look over to the distant campfire in the fool country on the other side where both the wise and the foolish have now become equally stupid, both heterosexuals and homosexuals have been exempted from the duty of reproduction, and everyone dances around the campfire until daybreak after toasting the "juice." You aspire to that world, and I can understand.

Simultaneously, I oppose the act of not drinking the water on some illusory belief—the so-called heroism to save all humankind from doomsday. As the parable of *The Wise King* makes clear, it was the king who appeared to be mad in the eyes of the masses, as only he did not drink the water that deranged people. The penalty for the dissident ranges from exclusion to slaughter, from alienation to crusade. Therefore, you must make up your mind to sacrifice your life once you decide not to drink the water. You may be paraded before the execution, where onlookers who are incapable of distinguishing right from wrong will condemn you as the only corrupt devil not guided by God. Your name will be cursed by posterity in the history of the fool. You say you act beyond vanity; they ask who wants your salvation. Manchu issued the hair-cutting decree,[23] greatly protested by Han Chinese, when they invaded the central plains of China and overthrew the Ming Dynasty. As a result of the history, however, most Han

---

23   The hair-cutting decree orders Han men who keep their hair to cut it off, with the slogan "either cut your hair or cut your head," which is a cultural conquest.

Chinese changed their dress to the Manchu manner; those who did not do so were either killed or fled overseas. I am not asking you to be a traitor to your country, but to treasure the value of your life. I wish the thing you hold your ground on, even at the cost of your life, to be something more practical and irrevocable in compliance with your own rationality.

If you still resist conformity by not drinking the water like the others after reading the paragraphs above, I will then firmly defend your right not to drink. Moreover, I will prove that there is value rather than vanity in such unorthodox behavior. There are different reasons why people choose not to drink the water; this is the individual right of each and is justified for anyone to protect his/her own right from infringement.

Hegel (2017) defines right in *Elements of the Philosophy of Right* as, "any existence in general that is the existence of free will" (p. 58). Taking the right to choose as an example, any choice combines both the positive freedom to accept what is offered and the negative freedom to refuse what is offered, which is grounded in the indeterminacy of the I—the abstract thought of a pure I, with no content of its own except the formal capacity to select among given desires. In short, making a choice is similar to maintaining one's inner discipline and rationality.

The revelatory paragraphs above provide you with multiple opportunities to reflect if your choice (as a right) is rational, which resides in the reassurance of its conformity to reason. There are two possible causes of this result. First, your right is indeed rational in the objective sense. Second, your right is not completely rational; however, searching for the internal errors and loopholes is beyond the reach of your wisdom and capability. Therefore, it remains rational to do something you regard as most likely to be rational, given your limited intelligence and competence.

One might ask why we are outnumbered by the enemy on the other side if our choice is really justified. Hegel (2017) seeks to prove in *Elements of the Philosophy of Right* that violence is a special right, generated and rationalized by the free will of criminals through committing atrocities. Our punishment of criminals is grounded on respect for them as rational people of free will and special rights, thus dealing them with their own right—violence, as described in the proverb, "answer a fool according to his folly, lest he be wise in his own eyes." But what would happen if we extended the logic a little further: what if the accomplices of captured criminals succeed in a prison raid and set them free? Does that mean the right to use violence is justified once again? "Petty thieves are hanged but usurpers are crowned" (Zhuangzi, 1989, p. 38). We cannot judge whether a certain "right" is rational, lofty, or justified merely based on the outcome of exercising the right.

To me, there is nothing wrong in you asserting your rights after careful consideration, as there is no original sin in you as a human. Each individual acquires their own special rights either at birth or during their upbringing. Here is an extreme example. If you were an ogre, you would have developed as an ogre either by genetic mutation or due to being brought up by cannibals (let us suppose you are abandoned after birth and raised by cannibals); therefore, you take human cannibalism for granted. Now you are hunted down as the sworn enemy of humans. It is your fate, but not your fault, to be destroyed. It is the fault of such a cruel and unfair fate. I wish you would cry into the air before your execution, "Oh, fate! How cruel you are! Why have you created such an insignificant person as me with such a unique right, and cast me into the vast world where all are against me?" If you want to be the hero of doomsday, please be a guardian rather than a deserter of your inner discipline at the last minute. It is not humiliating to see you begging for mercy in front of the glittering knife of the butcher; it is rather jarring to hear you flatly denying your own right as a makeshift response out of utilitarian purpose.

We should learn to tolerate the existence of mavericks who refuse to drink the water and to respect their rights, even if today we are lucky enough to stand with the masses whose values do not systematically collide with mainstream requirements. As mentioned above, mutual understanding devoid of subjectivity is difficult, but it is the only thing we can and should try to achieve. A Chinese TV program focuses exclusively on psychological interviews with prisoners on death row. We would be disgusted by many of them because their atrocities have explicitly exposed the wickedness of human nature, despite benign circumstances. However, we might sympathize with others about their experiences and even understand their situations, because the flower of their evil bloomed in the abyss of despair, and the edge of their brutality was honed under the law of the jungle. Would we pardon them? No, we would not, yet we would feel responsible for their crimes and their deaths. It is us who failed to illuminate their world of shade with torches of hope; it is us who failed to implant goodwill in their inner selves. We should eliminate them, but what we need to wipe clean furthermore is the tragic world that breeds the darkness.

Renyuan Dong

Part Three
Aesthetics

Renyuan Dong

10
Beauty Skin Deep and Beauty to the Bone

Core Question: What is Beauty?

Guang'qian Zhu (2015) once created an exquisite metaphor about the essence of aesthetics:

> One could adopt three completely different attitudes toward an ancient pine—practical, scientific, or aesthetic. What the carpenter sees is simply a piece of wood whose worth is determined by its utility. He/She is busy working out how it could be used for housing or construction, and considering how to cut it, ship it, and sell it. What the scientist sees is an evergreen flowering plant with needle-like leaves and spherical fruit. He/She is busy categorizing it into a specific species of a specific family and comparing its similarities and differences with other pine trees. The artist does not set his/her mind on something else far away but fully and attentively appreciates its green color, its snaking branches, and its unrestrained vigorous spirit (p. 4).

However, not everyone has tastes as superb as the artist described by Guang'qian Zhu; in contrast, they may create many fantasies and claptraps with neither utilitarian nor artistic value. For example, some think it must be lonely for the pine to stand alone, so they plant a fir beside it for company—not to create a balanced and sustainable grove; others are dissatisfied with the straightness of the pine branches, so they tie the branches to a bent wire frame to make them grow crookedly—not with the intention of increasing its value in the flower market; still others believe in the idea of "the tree growing in the soil with its roots buried in the air" and find it a pity that only the "tip of the iceberg" is admired, so they ask someone to dig it up for a glimpse of the pine as a whole—not for the purpose of research.

We take it for granted that commercial practices (practical activities) aim to maximize utility, scientific practices aim to seek truth, and aesthetic practices aim to pursue beauty—as if these three attitudes have all developed clear guidelines in practice and are always pursued in a manner that aims to achieve the stated goals. However, the inconsequential and involuntary fantasies and claptraps described above could never be classed as commercial or scientific practices in any case; therefore, they are inevitably sorted into the realm of aesthetics. The only difference between "general aesthetics" and commerce or science is that "aesthetic judgments are free of any particular interest" (Kant, cited in Wenzel, 2008, p. 19). The utilitarianism inherent in commerce is self-evident, while the truth-seeking function of science in turn guides practice and eventually leads to an increase in social welfare. In contrast, behaviors of "general aesthetics"—beauty in the broad sense, regardless of aesthetic appreciation or artistic creation—do not bring direct and obvious utility to the participants. In other words, beauty in the broad sense possesses no value that can be patented or traded, and therefore is not diminished when shared. There are two reasons for people to possess something exclusively: First, some objects retain their utility for a long time so we can store them for future use, such as savings in the bank or durable tools in the warehouse. However, aesthetic utility persists for a very short time, as the sensory enjoyment generated by beauty is experienced at the same time as the appreciation of beauty itself. (Only in extreme cases would beauty continue to take effect after perception ceases, such as the Stendhal syndrome.[24]) Moreover, sensitivity to a specific beauty gradually diminishes as the frequency of the same aesthetic experience increases. Second, exclusive possession is important if an object is scarce and can rarely be regained if we lose it, such as scientific patents. However, beautiful objects for aesthetic appreciation are almost omnipresent. It is wiser to have new experiences to keep our senses fresh and sharp rather than staying with the same beauty, which may induce aesthetic fatigue.

---

24   A psychosomatic disorder that causes rapid heartbeat, dizziness, fainting, confusion, and occasional hallucinations when an individual experiences something of great personal significance, particularly art.

The non-utilitarian character of general aesthetics defines the scope of empirical objects of pure aesthetic judgement. First, food is excluded from the category of purely aesthetic objects or pure works of art due to its utility of satiety. A cuisine that excels in visual appearance and aroma could merely be regarded as a sculpture composed of foodstuffs. A pure and complete aesthetic judgement of food should include looking at it, smelling it, savoring it, and then spitting it out, which is far from gourmet tasting as it is actually practiced. Moreover, while sculpture is lauded as a purely aesthetic object, architecture, costume, and industrial design are depreciated to the combined products of aesthetic and commercial practice, even though all of them are three-dimensional creations. While poetry is lauded as a purely aesthetic object, political tracts, legal instruments, and scientific papers are depreciated as the combined products of aesthetic and commercial or scientific practices, even though all of them are written documents.

Finally, it is often difficult to decide whether certain objects are purely aesthetic or not. For example, utilitarian concerns, such as mate selection and child reproduction, lie behind our evaluation of people's facial appearance. Therefore, such an evaluation cannot be regarded as a purely aesthetic judgement. In contrast, paintings are pure artworks because they bring nothing other than visual enjoyment to the viewers. What about portraits then? Is the evaluation of facial appearance in portraits a purely aesthetic judgement? So as we can see, there is no doubt that those fantasies and claptraps about the ancient pine should be included in the realm of aesthetics, but it is questionable whether architecture, designer products, or portraits are purely aesthetic objects, even though the latter seem to exhibit much more beauty than the former in the traditional sense. General aesthetics posits the purity of incentive devoid of utilitarian interest behind the behavior and the works that result from the behavior. From this perspective, the opposite of beauty in the broad sense is not ugliness, but rather indifference (lack of care) and ceasing to work when the behavior itself has no utilitarian purpose.

However, we still need to respect the fact that some artistic creations, such as *The Jack Pine* by Tom Thomson or the verse, "Between broken rocks striking my root deep, I bite the mountain green and won't let go," by Ban'qiao Zheng (cited in Zhou, 2003, p. 249), are simply more beautiful than the aforementioned fantasies and claptraps, which are also aesthetic practices applied to the same object—the ancient pine. We can still make judgments about the aesthetic value of various purely aesthetic objects whose scope is defined by general aesthetics; in other words, we can make the traditional distinctions between beautiful works of art and ugly ones. In Nietzsche's radical words, the definition of "specific aesthetics"—beauty in the narrow sense—is that "all beauty stimulates reproduction, from the lowest sexuality to the highest spirituality" (Nietzsche, 1997b, p. 63). Humans make instinctive judgments about the beauty of objects that enhance the vitality of life and about the ugliness of objects that diminish the vitality of life. To be precise, beauty in the narrow sense does not directly stimulate reproduction; rather, it triggers sensory contemplation and enjoyment, which is otherwise impaired or even suppressed by ugliness. The biological essence of specific aesthetics is a feast that activates the hormones of the endocrine system to ultimately enhance the health, spirit, and vitality of the art appreciator. This is fundamentally in line with the *will-to-live* and enhances each individual's ability to survive. From this perspective, beauty is the unity of opposites being both utilitarian and non-utilitarian. The distinction that sets "general aesthetics" apart from commerce or science should therefore be refined as: Aesthetic judgment is free of any particular interest except pure sensory enjoyment.

We can understand contemporary art to a certain degree after explicating the concepts of general and specific aesthetics. From Marcel Duchamp's *Bicycle Wheel* (Fig. 10.1) to Meret Oppenheim's *Luncheon in Fur* (Fig. 10.2), artists no longer pursue superficial eye candy or sensory enjoyment, as is usually the case in the traditional realm of specific aesthetics. Instead, they expand the scope of general aesthetics by creating purely useless works without any utilitarian intent. They seek to prove that even a work that does not look beautiful can be classed as a purely aesthetic object simply because of its "uselessness." This practice, which encourages bizarre ideas and advocates the deconstruction of all existing aesthetic values, is a rebellion against the statement that, "humans do everything for a utilitarian purpose, and aesthetic practice is no exception." Thus, for the first time in art history, obscurantist nonsense rooted in the absence of clear purpose and eye broccoli breaking away from traditional aesthetic values are displayed in museums as art. However, the standard of art criticism has not slipped as far as we may fear. Take the installation art of *Readymades* by Duchamp as an example. Although *Bicycle Wheel* was well received by critics, other items in the collection did not receive as much attention and appraisal, as they were literally unmodified ready-mades. One could dig the earth with the shovel in the collection and hang his/her coat on the coat rack directly. Although Duchamp selected these daily items for display with outstanding taste, they remain objects that are products of both aesthetic and commercial practice due to their residual functions. As durable tools of procession values, they are weighed down too heavily by their discrete price tags to float up to the sacred palace of art in the air.

Figure 10.1. *Readymades: Bicycle Wheel* [Mounted metal wheel], Museum of Modern Art, New York. Source: Duchamp (1951).

Figure 10.2. *Object (The Luncheon in Fur)* [Fur-covered cup, saucer, and spoon], Museum of Modern Art, New York. Source: Oppenheim (1936).

If we focus on established concepts of specific aesthetics underlain by tradition, we find that preferences for some aesthetic concepts are universal, while others may vary from person to person. I raised the following examples in Part One, Truth: Humans tend to regard curves as more beautiful than straight lines, a colorful palette more appealing than a monochrome one, music more mellifluous than noise, and a prosperous life more pleasant than a wanting one, if uninfluenced by specific values.

The reason why humans favor curves over straight lines may be traced back to the memory of a uterus from one's infancy. Compared to rectilinear lines, curves may instill a softer, more protective feeling that continues to be preferred after infancy. The reason why humans favor colors over monochrome may be traced back to more ancient memories—when our ancestors still lived in a primitive, natural environment, where a colorful world represented daytime and the world cast in black-and-white meant that night had fallen. As a diurnal creature whose vision is limited in a monochrome world and whose audition is relatively weak, humans would have faced a higher risk from predators by night. Across generations, the mentality of looking forward to the colorful day and fearing the monochrome night would have become engrained in humans. The reason why humans favor music over noise simply reflects the fact that circumstances with rhythm or a relatively predictable course are preferable to unpredictable, chaotic alternatives; the former provides us with information we can use to act and therefore provides a greater sense of security than does the latter. Over the long centuries across which these ideas have been passed down, we have remembered only the conclusions (what is *beautiful* and what is *ugly*) and forgotten the reasons (because it is *beneficial* or *harmful* for human survival). In consequence, modern humans experience the conditioned reflex of sensory enjoyment when they are exposed to a stimulus that is beneficial for survival.

This ascription of the origin of aesthetic concept establishment to conflicts of interest in primitive human society is supported by evolutionary psychology. Evolutionary psychology views the emergence of modern civilization as occupying only a fraction of the span of human history; hence it does not affect the evolutionary direction of human beings or change evolutionary inertia from ancient times. (Agricultural societies emerged 5000 years ago and the industrial revolution occurred a mere 200 years ago. For 99% of human history, our ancestors lived in primitive hunter-gatherer tribes.) The modern human brain is still designed to solve the problems of survival that our ancestors faced. Therefore, cognition in the modern human brain is often slow to update and is similar to that of our ancestors, as if we have "stone-age minds in modern skulls" (Cosmides & Tooby, 1997, n.p.). A typical example that supports evolutionary psychology is our fanatical addiction to high-sugar, high-calorie food, which made sense in a primitive society that was chronically short of nutrients. During periods of hunger when extra nutritional supplement was always needed, our ancestors would not hesitate to run to a fruit tree and consume its high-sugar fruit. As modern society emerged with its excess availability of nutrition, food that is high in sugar and calories but empty of other nutrients is instead tagged as junk food, the extra intake of which may lead to health problems such as obesity, high cholesterol, and diabetes. Modern people have not evolved fast enough mentally to overcome these habitual addictions, which have already endangered health nowadays. In general, our deep-rooted concepts of gaining advantage and avoiding harm tend to be similar to that of our ancestors; thus, aesthetic concepts rooted in such common memory—named as the "primitive aesthetics"—tend to be universally appreciated by every different culture and race. Of course, there are always exceptions. Some people in modern society have ornithophobia, an abnormal and irrational fear of birds that may be related to a primitive memory of their ancestors who had been attacked by birds. Others suffer from trypophobia, as their ancestors may have witnessed corpses eaten away by large quantities of maggots. It is not surprising that the former cannot appreciate the slightest beauty in Picasso's *Dove of Peace*, while the latter can't help but scream in front of Yayoi Kusama's polka dots.

Despite the statement above that humans tend to regard curves as more beautiful than straight lines, a colorful palette more appealing than a monochrome one, music more mellifluous than noise, and a prosperous life more pleasant than a wanting one, that is not always the case. In fact, whenever we find a work of art that demonstrates the beauty of curves, colors, or rhythms, we can always find another that demonstrates the beauty of straight lines, monochrome, or even noise, as demonstrated in Figures 10.3-10.6.

Beauty of Curves

Figure 10.3. *The Source* [Oil on canvas], Musée d'Orsay, Paris. Source: Ingres (1856).

The Source is a masterpiece that displays the beauty of curves to the extreme: the plentiful figure of the female, the elegant curve-shaped pot, the meandering springs… There is almost no rectilinear element in the picture.

Beauty of Straight Lines

Figure 10.4. *Trafalgar Square* [Oil on canvas]. Museum of Modern Art, New York. Source: Mondrian (1939-43).

Trafalgar Square is a masterpiece that displays the beauty of straight lines to the extreme: the artist represents the avenues and buildings around Trafalgar Square by straight lines and patches of color to create a minimalist and refreshing style. It provides an abstract and innovative geometrical interpretation of the landscape.

Beauty of color

Figure 10.5. *The Fifer* [Oil on canvas], Musée d›Orsay, Paris. Source: Manet (1866).

The Fifer is one of the earliest works that is liberated from the sepia tones of Classicism and Neoclassicism. The artist boldly paints the background with bright turquoise, which contrasts sharply with the crimson, yellow, and white of the boy's outfit, creating a strong color impact on the viewers.

Beauty of Monochrome

Figure 10.6. *Migrant Mother* [Photograph], Museum of Modern Art, New York. Source: Lange (1936).

Migrant Mother captures the struggle to live of migrant workers during the Great Depression and the misery of their children. Although color photography had long since been invented when this image was captured, the photographer still chose the monochromatic tone to represent the sufferings of the Great Depression and people's pessimistic expectations of the future.

Beauty of Rhythms

Symphony No. 5 in C minor (van Beethoven, 1807-08/1960) is a masterpiece that displays the beauty of rhythm to the extreme. The agitated, repetitive opening gives the audience the impression that "fate is knocking at the door," and the following movements alternate between the mellow and the exhilarating, enhancing the sense of the impending destiny that we sometimes fight against and at other times accept.

Beauty of Noise

Flight of the Bumblebee (Rimsky-Korsakov, 1899-1900/2017) is not mellifluous from a purely musical perspective. The aesthetic value of the music lies in the violin's imitation of the high-frequency vibration of the flying bumblebee that requires superb skill, abundant stamina, and sophisticated cooperation between the solo violinist and the orchestra. Our appreciation of the sound in fact reveals our acknowledgement of the superb musical skills demonstrated in the performance, which is based on our sense of safety that the sound comes from an artistic performance rather than an actual bee attack.

We also develop an aesthetic preference for concepts opposite to primitive aesthetics under certain circumstances. I call such concepts "modern aesthetics," which do not originate from the common memory of our ancestors but are shaped by our specific background or social culture. So many countries, so many customs. Modern aesthetic concepts that have been shaped by different cultures are not as universally accepted as primitive aesthetic concepts. They may be appreciated by some and rejected by others. But in general, those who cherish memories of past glories and hold pessimistic expectations of the future tend to appreciate the beauty of black and white more than those who experience the present as a golden age. Those who have received a good musical education tend to appreciate the beauty of noise more than those who are not musically literate.

Social learning theory provides theoretical support for the emergence of modern aesthetic concepts. Social learning theory asserts that, in the process of the continuous improvement and accumulation of culture, the man-made social and cultural environment has long since replaced the natural environment as the primary living environment for people. Human choice has thus taken the place of natural selection and become the dominant power in human evolution through the selection and improvement of genes that support the interconnected evolution of culture and genes. Typical examples that support social learning theory include the continued production of lactase after weaning among societies with developed animal husbandry. Lactase is an important enzyme that is produced during infancy to digest breast milk, and it usually ceases after weaning. In societies with a long history of animal husbandry, however, many people continue to produce lactase into adulthood because their diet contains a significant proportion of dairy products. Lactase enables them to digest lactose more efficiently and fully absorb nutrients such as glucose and galactose from dairy products. The phenomenon of lactase production in adulthood is rarely seen in societies with less developed animal husbandry, which reflects different directions of genetic improvement influenced by different human civilizations. In contrast to evolutionary psychology, social learning theory asserts that changes in social culture lead to timely advances in mental capacities and conceptual cognition. Therefore, different cultures in different regions and times will give rise to rich and varied modern aesthetic concepts, which is somewhat similar to the concept of fashion.

While primitive aesthetics similarizes our aesthetics by drawing on our memories from common ancestors, modern aesthetics diversifies our aesthetics by drawing on a variety of cultural influences; while primitive aesthetics emphasizes the historical influences on the shaping of innate aesthetic concepts, modern aesthetics dwells on how contemporary cultural influences transform acquired aesthetic concepts. It is not solely our aesthetics but all our ideas that are shaped by the pull of two completely opposing forces such as identical vs. different, old vs. new, etc. One school of art criticism defends contemporary art by employing the paired concepts of primitive and modern aesthetics. The reason contemporary art is not well accepted by the general public is because the tastes of the audience still lag behind in the primitive aesthetic phase, while contemporary artists express more of the pioneering modern aesthetic concepts that they have developed from their individual background and specific cultural environment. Therefore, only the minority who have grown up in an environment similar to that of the artists' can understand and appreciate their work. It is difficult for most of the audience with different backgrounds to tune in to artists' individual aesthetics, which also proves the absence of universally acknowledged values in modern aesthetics.

Thus, which theory is correct, evolutionary psychology or social learning? One possible answer is that both might be correct. Perhaps genetic selection and improvement, as evolutionary psychology puts it, is an extremely long process and will not accelerate or mutate because of short-lived human civilizations. Cultural evolution may not be able to achieve essential genetic improvements, but it may be able to maximize the potential of existing genes and optimize gene expression through epigenetic modification[25], based on the fact that different phenotypes can be derived from the same genotype. Continuing production of lactase in one's adulthood may be an example of such epigenetic modification. Every person possesses the gene or genome that controls the production of lactase since each individual is able to produce it during infancy. Epigenetic modification switches a specific function of the gene on or off. In normal circumstances, epigenetic modification switches on the relevant gene's function of producing lactase while breastfeeding and switches it off after weaning. In societies with well-developed animal husbandry and a dairy-based diet, keeping the function switched on after weaning will undoubtedly reduce the burden on other digestive enzymes, thus greatly benefiting the individual's digestive system. Since this originally temporary epigenetic modification of the enzyme benefits the individual over the long run, it is consolidated and retained for a longer period. Therefore, animal husbandry does not select and improve the "lactase gene" (in fact, there may not even be a single gene solely for lactase production); that is, animal husbandry does not act to retain high quality, long-lived genes and screen out inferior ones that cannot produce lactase after a period. Animal husbandry simply extends the length of time the gene expresses the specific function of producing lactase through epigenetic modification of the relevant gene or genome.

However, in some situations, the power of primitive memory far outweighs contemporary culture in shaping human ideas, as demonstrated by an example from aesthetics: people have a congenital and physiological aversion to the sound of fingernails scratching a blackboard. The influence of such "primitive ugliness" is so ingrained that no modern culture from any region or any time can change people's opinions about the sound from ear piercing to mellifluous. One possible explanation of this congenital aversion is that it resembles the sound of beasts crushing the skulls of our primitive ancestors (Xiong, 2017). Our ancestors had been the prey of beasts for countless years during primitive times. When a tiger crushed

---

25   Epigenetic modification refers to the reversible regulation of gene expression through DNA methylation, histone modification, and non-coding RNAs, such as miRNAs. Such regulation does not cause changes in gene sequences but can still be passed on to successive generations.

their skulls with one bite, rubbed its teeth against the human skeleton and sucked the bone marrow rapaciously, it generated the same sound as fingernails on a blackboard. Whenever our ancestors heard a sound at that pitch, they knew that one of their fellows had been hunted down by a nearby beast. They could avoid the dangerous area and guarantee their survival by establishing a physiological aversion to the sound. This judgement of ugliness has been consolidated as a conditioned reflex over the long course of evolution and remains today, even when beasts are no longer a threat.

We can draw two conclusions from the example above: First, an aesthetic judgement based on auditory information is much more influential than a judgement based on visual information. Humans receive 90% of external information through visual images and the remaining 10% through the other sensory channels, including hearing. Therefore, the human body must deliberately reduce its susceptibility to visual stimuli (or its susceptibility would diminish naturally when exposed to large quantities of visual images) to ensure that the body responds calmly/optimally to any visual information without becoming over-excited. In contrast, an aesthetic judgement based on auditory information is treated with more attention, as it is not buried in a sea of other auditory spam. Secondly, a judgement of beauty derived from primitive aesthetics can be easily overthrown by a judgement from modern aesthetics, and modern culture can even create unlikely aesthetic concepts that have been ignored by traditional primitive aesthetics. However, a judgement of ugliness derived from primitive aesthetics cannot be so easily overturned by modern civilization. In essence, primitive beauty merely adds to the welfare of human survival, whereas primitive ugliness warns us of dangerous factors that may have threatened the survival of our ancestors. The level of attention and compliance we pay to the two are completely different.

In addition to purely aesthetic concepts that arouse only sensory enjoyment, such as an appreciation of straight lines, monochrome, and noise, modern culture produces practical aesthetic concepts that imply specific cultural values and utilitarian concerns. Examples of such "utilitarian aesthetic concepts" include the combined products of aesthetics and commercial practice mentioned earlier. Take the body shape as an example: during the Tang Dynasty in ancient China, people appreciated women with plentiful figures as implying fertility; in the later Song Dynasty, people developed an opposite aesthetic that appreciated the skinny figures of females as representing femininity and weakness. Likewise, in Britain, one of the important signs that defined a handsome and noble man during the industrial revolution was delicate white skin, but men with healthy complexions are more appreciated nowadays. Such aesthetic reversals are all oriented by specific social values. During and after the Industrial Revolution in Britain, those who worked outdoors became brown and weather-beaten, and delicate white skin was the sign of the pampered bourgeoisie and the nobility who controlled wealth and power. Today, manual labor has largely been replaced by mental labor as the mainstream work mode of the society. Everyone has become an office worker and white skin is no longer rare. Instead, a healthy tanned complexion implies that the person is rich enough to take holidays abroad on some tropical island far away from overcast England. Although the aesthetic judgement has been overturned by 180 degrees, the social imperative to despise the poor and curry favor with the rich remains the same. Therefore, we can see that the gorgeous robe of beauty is often borrowed to conceal dishonorable and snobbish social values. Once pure aesthetics are contaminated by utilitarian values, it is hard to say that such aesthetic judgements are free from any particular interest.

We tend to regard "primitive aesthetic concepts" as "purely aesthetic concepts" that are conceptual and without utilitarian value, or rather the utilitarian value has long been forgotten over the centuries of memory-inheritance. In contrast, "modern aesthetic concepts" contain many "utilitarian aesthetic concepts" with a specific value orientation. However, these two groups of concepts are not in a strict one-to-one correspondence with each other. It is best to test whether a particular aesthetic concept belongs to primitive aesthetics, modern aesthetics, pure aesthetics, or utilitarian aesthetics with an infant who has not yet acquired social norms. Utilitarian concerns, such as mate selection and child reproduction, are concealed behind our evaluation of people's facial appearance. Therefore, our evaluation should be classed as within the scope of utilitarian aesthetics. Meanwhile, various studies have shown that infants are more excited by pictures of handsome men and beautiful women than photographs of ordinary looking people; neural activity in their respective cerebral cortices is noticeably more excited. The aesthetic evaluation of people's appearance, and its implied reproductive concern, has already been engraved deeply into human instincts and genes; thus, it falls into the realm of primitive aesthetics.

Figure 10.7 shows to which quadrant, between primitive and modern aesthetics and between pure and utilitarian aesthetics, each aesthetic concept belongs. The aesthetics of tragedy, which appears in the top right quadrant, are discussed in depth in the final chapter of this part.

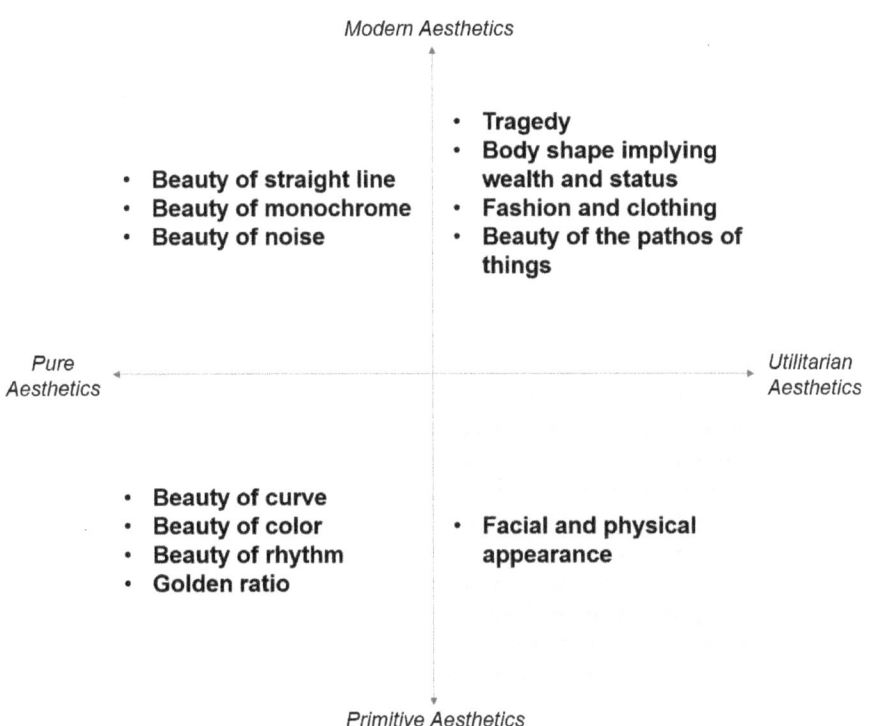

Figure 10.7. The Four Quadrants of Aesthetics.

Renyuan Dong

11
At the End of What You Should Know Is the Beginning of What You Should Sense

Core Question: What is Art?

Artwork is a medium for beauty. Yet artwork has often involved more than simply beauty in its historical evolution. The development of Chinese ink-wash painting has evolved from pursuing pure beauty to combining that pursuit with a quest for an accurate depiction of the art object. The expressive freehand style[26] of Chinese painting originated among highly educated scholars and the literati, whose leisure time allowed them to develop a special taste and a pure aesthetic of brushstrokes and ink. While the former implies a utilitarian aesthetic of particular morals, such as open-mindedness and internal peace, the latter pursues the pure aesthetic of solely sensory pleasure. At the stage of rendering pure beauty, the artists paid more attention to the degree of force needed in the application of brushstrokes, the ratio of water to ink, and the cultivation of concrete or void conceptions than to similarities in form between the depicted objects and their artistic interpretations. The meticulous realist style[27] of Chinese painting that matured between the Tang and the Song Dynasties was a

---

26 Also known as *Xieyi* painting, where *Xieyi* means "sketching thoughts" in Chinese, which involved watercolor or brushstroke painting.

27 Also known as *Gongbi* painting, where *Gongbi* means "meticulous brush craftsmanship" in Chinese, a technique using highly detailed brushstrokes that delimit details very precisely.

much later development than the freehand style. It was often practiced by court painters and sought to vividly reproduce the appearance of an object through the meticulous depiction of its details to express formal resemblances. It was a step onward from the idealized resemblances of the freehand style. However, despite the detailed craftsmanship of the meticulous style, Chinese painting still lagged behind Western painting in terms of technically sophisticated and accurate depictions of objects. This was because aesthetic practices in China had never been subject to a systematic study of how to depict objects in nature realistically, resulting in an absence of perspective theory describing the spatial relationship among different objects. For example, objects at different distances from the viewer were usually depicted at the same scale in Chinese painting; even when nearby objects were depicted as bigger and objects far away as smaller, they were not in strict proportion to each other. A knowledge of shading techniques for creating the illusion of a three-dimensional object on a two-dimensional canvas was also absent. The consequent lack of shadows and highlights flattened objects in Chinese paintings. This remained the case until the early Qing Dynasty, when the Italian Jesuit missionary Giuseppe Castiglione (1688-1766) came to China and served as a court painter. He introduced scientific painting techniques from the West that influenced traditional ink-wash paintings, leading to a culmination of Chinese painting that embraced the realistic depiction of painted objects while retaining traditional Chinese aesthetic values.

Figure 11.1. *Eight Horses* [Hanging scroll, ink and color on silk], The Palace Museum, Beijing. Source: Castiglione, Giuseppe aka Lang, Shining (1723-35).

Castiglione's masterpiece, *Eight Horses* (Fig. 11.1), takes the traditional Chinese theme of horses as the subjects of the picture and vividly depicts the three-dimensional stature of each horse, as well as the spatial relationships among them.

In contrast to the development of Chinese painting, Western painting progressed from the pursuit of realistic depiction, with ornamentation as a lesser concern to the pursuit of pure beauty (before the rise of contemporary art movements such as Dadaism and Pop Art). Western painters were initially employed by Popes, bishops, and nobles to create religious works and portraits that had clear utilitarian functions. Portraits needed to faithfully record the appearance (and often the significance) of the subject for the sake of posterity; religious works needed to create concrete images of religious figures and their settings to assist the faithful in visualizing and tuning in to their heroic deeds. Western painting achieved a considerable allegorical and documentary function before the invention of photography. Thus, it is unsurprising that artists of the Classical to the Neoclassical periods continually honed techniques for realistic representation, combined with decorative elements that either hinted at the temperament of the sitter of the portrait or cloaked a mythological figure in sanctity.

Later, with the movement of Romanticism, paintings were liberated from the strictly prescribed themes set out above. Artwork grew more diverse, commenting on the present while focusing on the past; valuing emotion, individualism, and nature while incorporating fantasy, legend, and exoticism—all set against the backdrop of the decline of the aristocracy and religious authority in European life, advancements in scientific technologies, and the diversification of social classes. Romantic works examine the lives of emerging classes, depict the influence of industrial development on society, and explore the exotic cultures of other nations brought to Europe by exploration and trade. Although paintings of this period made several breakthroughs in color and brushstroke, they did not renounce the realistic depiction of nature. Instead, on top of being beautiful and technically accomplished, artworks of this time became even more utilitarian, since these diverse themes reflected many social issues and addressed the specific interests of the artists.

It was not until the advent of *L'art pour l'art* (art for art's sake)[28] in the early 19th century that Western painting gradually gave up its obsession with realistic depiction through the successive explorations made by Impressionism (representatives: Van Gogh and Monet), Symbolism (representative: Mondrian), Cubism (representative: Picasso), Surrealism (representative: Dali) and Abstract Expressionism (representative: Jackson Pollock). While in the period of Impressionism, artists no longer sought

---

28 *L'art pour l'art* asserted that the only "true" art has no moral, utilitarian, or didactic function. It eventually led to the aesthetic revolution to abandon realistic depictions in paintings and pursue pure beauty.

to faithfully reproduce the objective appearances of the depicted objects, but rather to integrate their subjective impressions and emotions into their representation of the scene before them. By the advent of Abstract Expressionism, artists completely abandoned external shapes and forms and shifted their enthusiasm to the creation of sheer visual sensations with pigments and brushstrokes, which coincides with the pursuit of pure beauty through an expressive style, an initial phase in the development of Chinese painting. As we can see, Western painting has gradually discarded the extra burdens of being scientific and realistic (art for documentation or the sake of other functions) and returned to the source of being solely beautiful (art for art's sake) through its historical development.

The diametrically reversed processes of the development of Chinese and Western aesthetics are also evident in other fields. For example, China invented gunpowder for celebratory firecrackers by as early as the Tang Dynasty, but no one thought to investigate its properties and refine it into a powerful military explosive. The technology of gunpowder passed to the West through wars between Mongolians and Arabs, and later between Arabs and Europeans. It was not until 1867 that Nobel invented TNT, a more potent and stable form of dynamite. After decades of refinement, TNT and its derivatives became the most lethal weapons on the battlefield and expanded the gap in military capacity between the East and the West. In a sense, China lacked the haste in scientific and commercial practice that characterized its Western counterparts and showed more grace in maintaining purely aesthetic and post-utilitarian practices.

The evaluation of a work of art depends on two aspects: its apparent aesthetic value and its internal connotation or philosophy. According to Nietzsche's aesthetic theory, the former is the beautiful illusion of the object's exterior in the light of Apollo, while the latter is the reflection of the essence of life after eradicating exterior illusions under the guidance of Dionysus. Lovers of contemporary art often criticize traditional art as concerning itself only with creating sensory pleasure, exemplified by superficial eye candy in paintings. Yet masterpieces of any period must possess a seamlessly integrated aesthetic appearance outside and profound content inside, such that the content sinks into the viewers' minds naturally when they marvel at the gorgeous robe of the appearance. The entire process of message delivery takes place so effortlessly that it has not even been noticed by the viewers themselves. This contrasts with the common misreading of Euripides' statement, "To be beautiful, everything must be intelligible," as if one needs first to stare at a piece of art, thoroughly inspect it, and invent some opinionated interpretation of the work before one can claim that he/she is able to appreciate the beauty of the work.

Figure 11.2. *Entrance to the Harbor* [Oil on canvas]. Museum of Modern Art, New York. Source: Seurat (1888).

Figure 11.3. *Sunday Afternoon on the Island of La Grande* [Oil on canvas], Art Institute of Chicago, Chicago. Source: Seurat (1884).

Rainstorm of Tomorrow

For example, the neo-impressionist painter Georges-Pierre Seurat invented pointillism. The landscapes and characters in his works are all composed of tiny dots of precise color (much like the concept of pixels today), and the multitude of dots give the whole picture a harmonious and uniform appearance (see Figures. 11.2 and 11.3). Through this aesthetic practice, the artist seeks to convey the scientific concept that everything in the world is made up of physical particles such as atoms. If you move a little closer to the picture, the exterior shape of an object as a whole vanishes and the viewer is left with a bunch of colorful dots adjacent to each other. The greatest advantage of Seurat's painstaking technique of arranging dots of complementary colors together is its ability to capture subtle color variations in different details of the picture and to depict the ever-changing world with the instantaneous colors cast by the varying light. Furthermore, although the distribution of gas molecules in the air is extremely sparse, the artist does not abandon his densely dotted brushstrokes even when depicting empty space, as if to imply the omnipresence of photons with the property of physical particles—or traditionally, the light.

Figure 11.4. *The Persistence of Memory* [Oil on canvas], Museum of Modern Art, New York. Source: Dali (1931).

Another example of the seamless integration of aesthetic appearance and internal philosophy is Dali's surrealist masterpiece *The Persistence of Memory*, which successfully creates a mysterious atmosphere of absurdity by melting and twisting the shapes of clocks and watches—in contrast to their stereotype of being firm and rigid (Fig. 11.4). Freudianism and the theory of a subconscious mind behind such an aesthetic appearance are also evident: the melted and twisted clocks symbolize the way in which memories are gradually distorted over time. The pocket watch closest to the viewer is even covered with foraging ants, suggesting that the more distant the memory, the more severe the corruption. The only explicitly concrete image in the entire picture is the façade of mountains and coastline in the background, the Catalonian landscape where Dali spent his childhood. The artist thus expresses the message that although many memories fade as time flows on, childhood memories related to one's hometown are deeply rooted and persistently influence his/her future development.

Correspondingly, contemporary art, especially works of performance and installation art, often abandons the creation of an appearance of "skin-deep" beauty and focuses more on building and communicating the so-called "more profound" philosophical connotations of the work. This adds to the viewers' confusion about how to evaluate the work: how can I tell that the artist is not putting together a pile of junk to fool me and then trying to impose some pretentious thoughts and connotations on the work? After all, it is much easier to attach an exaggerated promotional explanation to work than to create a work of art that is rich in intrinsic beauty. We acknowledge aesthetic practices such as the *Bicycle Wheel* of Marcel Duchamp and the *Object* (*Luncheon in Fur*) of Meret Oppenheim as pioneering works that challenge traditional and narrow-minded aesthetic judgements that regard only beautiful things as aesthetic. Their works provide us with the possibility that the unassuming Cinderella can also be the child of Aphrodite. However, the revolution that helped art to surpass simple beauty seems to have gone too far. Being beautiful seems to be shameful today, and beauty is supplanted by nonsensical theories. With such fanaticism, audiences are exposed to many inferior duplicates of Duchamp's and Oppenheim's works whenever they stroll into a modern art museum nowadays. Art practices such as Dadaism and Pop Art should have "fallen at the hurdle" after several precautious, satiric, and innovative works emerged, but they did not.

Imagine you are a young graduate of an art academy and are struggling to make ends meet. There are two paths before you: on one side echo the insurmountable masterpieces of the past in pursuit of pure aesthetics, together with the increasingly demanding critics of the masses who have received the baptism of those works; on the other side stand the flubdubs, such as a urinal with a signature on it or a print of Marilyn Monroe's portrait framed in gold, wrapped in their mantles of esteem rooted in the popular psychology of seeking novelty. Which way would you turn? Take a step back: if a great work with profound connotations but an unimpressive presentation really exists, its value would be overwhelmed by countless bad works with equally unimpressive presentation created by frivolous and snobbish peers. This is like a treasure in a slum. It is generally believed that there are no treasures in the slums, as any that existed would have been looted by the slum's residents, and anyone who acquires wealth would spend money repairing their house instead of retaining the appearance of a slum. Therefore, even today there are treasures hidden in deserted slums that are exempted from looting due to non-inhabitancy. The public may have no interest in organizing a treasure hunt inside the slum due to their prejudices about the appearance and their stereotypes about slums.

Of course, contemporary art is not full of works that are poorly presented. There are artworks with both an aesthetic appearance outside and a profound connotation within. However, it is often the case that the two are not intimately integrated or even fragmented. As a consequence, the audience *cannot* completely understand or may even *misread* the message of the work through pure aesthetic appreciation without the assistance of any narrative about its inspiration and connotations. Of course, good art should speak for itself rather than relying on narrative for justification.

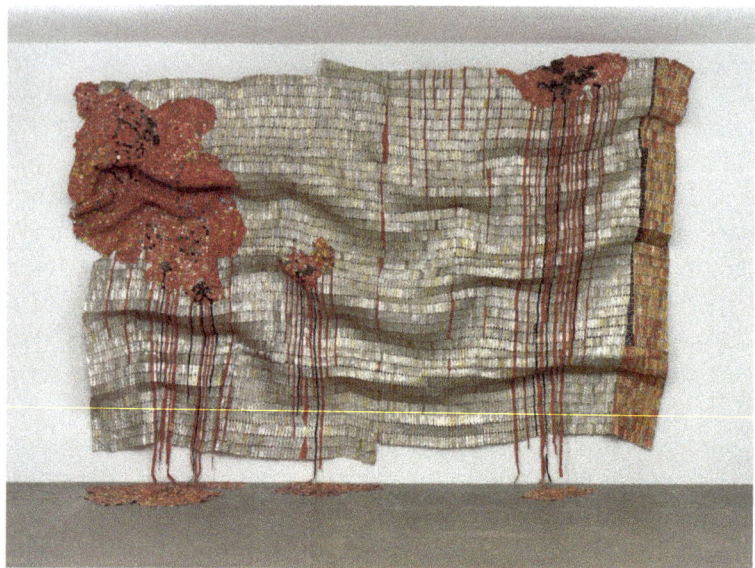

Figure 11.5. *Bleeding Takari II* [Bottle caps, seals, and copper wire], Museum of Modern Art, New York. Source: Anatsui (2007).

Bleeding Takari II is a shimmering tapestry woven from beer bottle caps and seals, not ordinary wool (Figure 11.5). The blood on the tapestry and the pool of blood on the ground are made from red bottle caps and seals, respectively. This work of art reflects the bloody history of the slave trade in the artist's home country of Nigeria during the period of colonization by Europe and America. The large bloodstain on the left side of the tapestry forms the shape of Nigeria, while the bloodstain at the work's top-right corner symbolizes the tip of Europe that took slaves from the country. At the time, European colonialists bartered for African slaves with beer; later, alcohol became the currency and the medium of trade in slave markets. The magnificent appearance of the work, which symbolizes the European colonialists and African lords who profited from the slave trade, echoes the blood shed by the slaves from the colony and the beer that became both the witness and the symbol of this cruel history.

Figure 11.6. *Untitled (Night Train)* [Glass, silicone glue, and coal], Museum of Modern Art, New York. Source: Hammons (1989).

Untitled (Night Train) is a sculpture with a glittering, emerald-like appearance (Figure 11.6). Parallel-packed beer bottles resemble a railroad track or closely packed train carriages, while the gravel at the bottom of the sculpture reinforces the symbolism of the railway. In fact, the railway has always been an inseparable part of the fate of African-Americans. As early as the Westward Expansion, many African slaves were trafficked into the United States for forced labor laying railway tracks; at the time of American Civil War, southern slaves stole onto night trains to escape to the freedom of the North, travelling on the railway lines laid by their ancestors; even in America today, where slavery has long been abolished, the train is still the preferred means of economic travel for many African-Americans. The artist collected many empty bottles of Night Train and Thunderbird beer (low-cost brands that specifically target African-Americans) near railways or in African-American neighborhoods as a visual symbol of the close relationship among the railway, alcohol, and African-American life. The artist uses the beer bottles of cheap brands that target African-Americans to build a sculpture symbolizing the railway, thereby reflecting both the railway-centered history of slavery and rebellion as well as creating a metaphor for the exclusion and exploitation of the African-American community from mainstream economic life. This remains the case even though slavery was abolished long before 1989, when the work was created, as evidenced by their economic means of travel and their cheap drinks.

Both of the contemporary sculptures and installations discussed above are related to the theme of slavery in Europe and America. The audience is required to process the following three issues simultaneously to accurately understand the messages behind the works: They must understand the identity of African-Americans and Europeans to detect the theme of slavery; they must be familiar with the slave trade across Africa, Europe, and America and the tragic suffering of African slaves; and they must have some knowledge of alcohol in African culture to read the connotations of the bottle caps and seals. Audiences who can accurately understand the ideology of the works across all three dimensions are rare. Many white audiences who know little about the history of slavery and beer culture could easily misread the theme of the two sculptures as waste recycling or environmental protection, not to mention Asian audiences who drift away from such history. Compared with classic art, contemporary art is more ambitious in expressing the artist's own idea or message through the work. Georges-Pierre Seurat invented Pointillism to illustrate that everything in the world is composed of physical particles, and Salvador Dali made *The Persistence of Memory* to illustrate the distortion of memory over time. Yet the themes of *Bleeding Takari II* and *Untitled (Night Train)* cannot be summarized in a single sentence. They reveal a slice of history, the story of a certain community, and its intricate interrelations with history through the symbols of the past. However, the works feature too much ideological information for audiences of different backgrounds to universally understand them in an epiphany or enlightenment at the moment when they marvel at the apparent aesthetics, just as one seeks to write the *Koran* on a piece of gorgeous robe and discovers the size of the fabric is insufficient to include all narratives. I call such phenomena, "the overload of the core."

The reason for the "overload of the core" is that each form of artistic expression has its own advantages and limitations. For example, painting is an art of concretion. It is very good at rendering figurative objects, but it is extremely difficult to show the flow of time in a still picture. In fact, all paintings that express time as their theme show the phenomenon of time passing through its impact on concrete objects, rather than time itself. For example, Dali's *The Persistence of Memory* shows the eroding effect of time on the clocks that represent memory; Duchamp's *Nude Descending a Staircase* records the trajectory of the nude descending the stairs as time flies by. Music, in contrast, is an art of process. It is very good at expressing the flow of time and eliciting the audience's emotions; it would be more accurate to say that the performance of any piece of music must be accompanied by the flow of time. However, music would struggle to express figurative objects and detailed plots. While we have musical compositions, such as *Romeo and Juliet* and the *Sleeping Beauty Waltz* by Tchaikovsky, to tell us stories through music, the majority of the audience is not able to associate the music they hear with the plot of the story, except for audience members with considerable music literacy and ample prior acquaintance with the story. Literature, on the other hand, can express not only figurative objects but also the flow of time. In addition, it can achieve what music cannot: flashbacks in time. Poetry such as *Still You Linger by My Side* creates a chronological journey in reverse to familiar objects and daily scenes from childhood, giving the reader a unique experience.

> Still You Linger by My Side[29]
>
> The water of the cataract flowed upwards,
> The seeds of the dandelion, flung afar, slowly reformed into a little umbrella,
> The sun rose in the west and slowly sank to the east.
>
> Back went the flare to the gun barrel,
> Athletes returned to the starting line,
> Putting down the admission notice, I forgot decades of hard study.
>
> From the kitchen came the savor of meals,
> You signed your name on my test paper,
> The TV was turned off, my schoolbag handed over,
>
> You were still by my side.

Whenever the artistic ideology or philosophical connotations the artist wishes to convey goes beyond the capacity of a specific medium of artistic expression, he/she will seek to integrate different artistic media (often called multimedia art) to deliver a more complex message. Songs, whether in opera at the theater or in the form of folk music, are the product of close

---

29   *Still You Linger by My Side* is a poem by Chang Dai during his study at The Chinese University of Hong Kong, expressing his loneliness from being separated from his mother.

cooperation between pure music and poetry. In many modern art museums, multimedia art combines dynamic videos or still pictures with music or narration. You may think of them as experimental art films addressed to the minority. However, multimedia art of any kind, whether songs or movies, is dominated by literature and the ideology it conveys, whereas painting and music are reduced to the subordinate position of mere decoration. Language can accurately express any context or content due to its incomparable flexibility. Its only drawback is that it needs to be understood before it can trigger the intrinsic sensibility of the aesthetic subject, which is much less efficient than painting or music that can directly stimulate the sensory channels to instantly arouse aesthetic feelings. If we deconstruct multimedia art, we find that the meaning of a song can be fully conveyed by its lyrics, but the lyrics alone are not enough to arouse the emotional sensations of the audience. That is why we need to compose music to accompany the words. Likewise, we would find that the story of a film can be fully conveyed in the novel, but the text itself is not sufficiently figurative to provide the audience with an immersive experience. That is why we need to supplement the words with the screenplay. To some extent, multimedia art combined with literature has helped to popularize and generalize the aesthetics of daily life. After all, most audiences are pragmatists who prefer spending two hours in a movie with a clear theme to wandering around an unintelligible art exhibition for an entire afternoon. The classic screenshots and soundtracks of a movie have more chance of exposure to the public than art exhibitions or concerts with higher aesthetic requirements. On the other hand, when painting and music become mere accessories to literature, they are no longer treated seriously as purely aesthetic objects—or shall we say that purely aesthetic practice has lost its position in modern life bustling with utilitarian pursuits.

12

The Thousand-Faceted Aphrodite

Core Question: Is There a Standard Aesthetic Paradigm Guaranteeing the Beauty of Artworks in Accordance with It?

Humans have always sought a paradigm for behavior such that actions consistent with the paradigm are considered ethical and those violating the paradigm are considered evil. This search has led to utilitarianism. I described in detail how utilitarianism results in different behavior under different circumstances in Part Two, Ethics. Overall, however, achieving the greatest good for the greatest number is still a necessary and sufficient condition of ethics. Likewise, humans have always sought an aesthetic paradigm for art (e.g. the concept of the golden ratio) such that artworks consistent with the paradigm are judged as beautiful, and artworks violating the paradigm are judged as ugly. In earlier aesthetic theories, philosophers proposed many preconditions for the birth of beauty—though adhering to such preconditions did not guarantee beauty—as necessary conditions of aesthetics, as well as many typical characteristics of beauty as sufficient conditions of aesthetics—though instances of beauty lacking such characteristics could exist. It seems difficult for us to find an equivalent definition of beauty today, except from the biological perspective, which defines beauty as external stimuli that trigger sensory pleasure, thereby enhancing the vitality of the aesthetic subject. (In other words, it is hard for us to summarize the kinds of external stimuli that are capable of triggering sensory pleasure.) Aesthetics is difficult to define because of its infinite possibilities and boundless potential.

Instead, we can give three explanations as to why the standard aesthetic paradigm for judging the beauty or ugliness of an artwork is so flexible, indescribable, or even non-existent. First, an evaluation of the aesthetic value of an artwork is influenced by the psychology of the aesthetic subject. The audience will consider the medium of artistic expression (painting, photography, sculpture, music, etc.) employed in each artwork and alter their judging criteria accordingly. In general, audiences tend to appreciate and affirm the value of art that required significant effort to produce, regardless of the expressive form it takes. We may know that a work that requires many hours to complete in one medium may be easily accomplished in another. If it were created as a commercial practice, the former would be rejected as inefficient. However, evaluations of the commercial value and the aesthetic value of the same object tend in opposite directions. Aphrodite would acknowledge the effort the artist puts into the work because aesthetic judgment is devoid of any particular interest and somehow opposes the "utilitarian first" approach. An audience would appreciate a realistic painting vivid with life that required a large amount of painstaking effort to complete, but largely ignore an equally realistic photograph that had been created by the mere closing of a shutter (if the photograph demonstrates no strength other than being realistic).

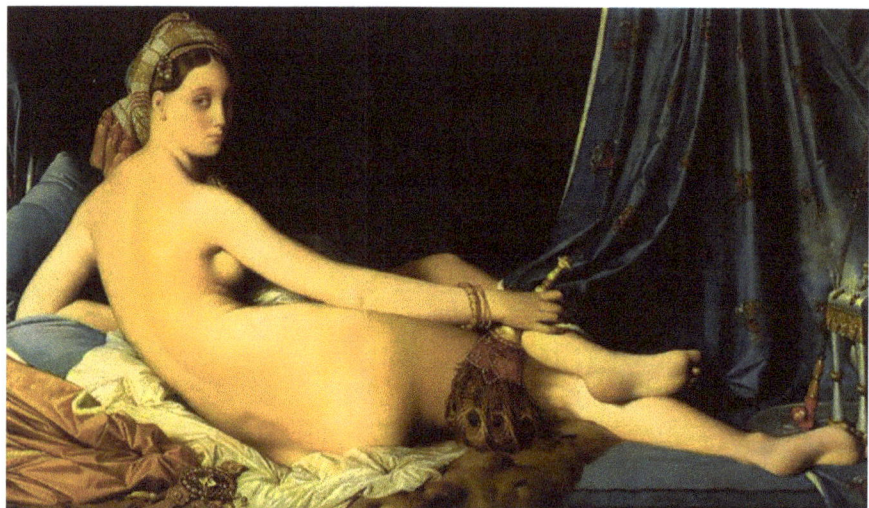

Figure 12.1. *Grande Odalisque* [Oil on canvas]. Louvre, Paris. Source: Ingres (1814).

Take *Grande Odalisque* as an example (Figure 12.1). This painting aroused great controversy and criticism when first exhibited in Paris. The art critic de Kératry once told Ingres's student Amaury-Duval, "His Odalisque has three [lumbar] vertebrae too many," while Amaury-Duval retorted, "De Kératry might be correct. And so what? It is the very long soft waistline that makes the Odalisque lure the audience at first sight. If the proportions of the figure were absolutely accurate, she might not be as attractive" (Maigne, 2004, p. 342). Today, Ingres's *Grande Odalisque* is regarded as a classic because she is an artistic image that is inspired by life but goes beyond it. *Grande Odalisque* is generally realistic, but her neck, back, and pelvis have been deliberately lengthened by the artist to make her surpass all real women and rise to the image of a muse that exists only in art. Now, imagine if *Grande Odalisque* were not carefully painted by hand but were instead a camera shot of a posed female model and background settings, which had then undergone some post-processing by Photoshop or other photo editing software to lengthen the neck, back, and pelvis of the figure. Would this hypothetical artwork be as sensational as the painting? Probably not, because the post-shoot editing is no more than an ordinary, standard step for a medium whose essential realism has been guaranteed. On the contrary, it is difficult enough for an artist to be sufficiently skilled to depict objects realistically; however, Ingres did not stop there but went further to idealize an image that was already true to life. The audience may suddenly realize that the figure in the painting is superior to any real being because of her idealized body proportions before they are almost convinced and mistake the Odalisque as a real woman due to her lifelike depiction. *Grande Odalisque* is a window that connects the real world with the ideal world, refreshing our sensual experience with an image that seems to be simultaneously at our fingertips and yet unapproachable.

The tendency for the audience to appreciate the value of art that has been created with devoted effort also explains the unpopularity of contemporary art, as the latter pursues the sparkle of inspiration and effortlessness in its presentation, although at times the creative idea of the work results from long contemplation by the artist and may not be as effortless as it looks. It is unsurprising that there are still many audiences who cannot link beauty with easily made objects, such as an inverted bicycle wheel on a stool or a teacup coated with fur, no matter how we interpret the pioneering spirit of Duchamp and Oppenheim's artistic practices.

The second explanation of the flexibility (or the indescribable nature) of the standard aesthetic paradigm is that it requires us to create unfamiliarity in the familiar world and cultivate unknown wonders in the fields already known. Beauty must be yielded in an environment of safety and familiarity, because aesthetic practice is free of any particular interest and therefore can emerge only after practices that have a specific interest such as the pursuit of knowledge or utility. Humans must follow the sequence of pursuing "truth," "ethics," and only then "aesthetics" in their exploration of the external world and must not interrupt the order by will. Imagine yourself as the astronaut in the movie *Interstellar*. You have reached a remote planet whose entire surface is covered by an ankle-depth layer of seawater, which is quite breathtaking, is it not? However, the first thing you need to do is conduct scientific research into the strange environment, not admire the landscape in front of you. Otherwise, you will lose your life the next moment in the thousand-meter-high waves generated by the huge gravitational field of a nearby planet, as depicted in the movie. The primary goal of human practice when facing an unfamiliar environment or a new object is to seek truth—to obtain knowledge about the unknown through a scientific approach—and to use such knowledge to increase one's chances of survival. Only when we have enough knowledge of the external world so that it no longer threatens human survival will it be reclassified from unknown to known: a condition that indicates a greater sense of safety. The goal of human activity in this safe phase shifts to maximizing utility—to utilize and transform the familiar environment to gain more resources and a better life. In the same example above, once the astronaut acquired sufficient understanding of the giant tides (e.g. knowledge about the tide table and affected regions) and defensive measures were in place (e.g. docking in the underground basement or hovering in space when the tide arrived), the astronaut might employ the huge waves to generate hydropower, then use the electricity to decompose the seawater for oxygen, and eventually transform the planet into a human-friendly habitat. Only after all of this is completed will we have the leisure to appreciate the beauty of the planet. Beauty is a leisure product born in a carefree environment where a sense of safety is guaranteed by scientific research and abundant resources are produced by utilitarian practice. Therefore, such a superior and interest-free activity usually comes into practice after the two.

Euripides' statement that, "To be beautiful, everything must be intelligible" is a partial encapsulation of the second explanation. In fact, strange and unknown objects leave the audience in confusion and with feelings of absurdity, which hinders them from asserting a clear judgement on the beauty or ugliness of the object. Such feelings of absurdity reflect our conservative and defensive stance toward novelties due to our sense of insecurity, which in turn encourages us to research the unknown objects for a thorough understanding, instead of leaping to a biased aesthetic judgement of objects that are not yet comprehended.

Figure 12.2. An Early Artwork Created Using Google DeepDream. Source: Thoma (2015).

Most audiences would find this picture (Figure 12.2), which has been created by Google DeepDream,[30] an AI algorithm that simulates human neural networks, strange or confusing, rather than beautiful or ugly. The overly complicated patterns and bizarrely integrated shapes created by artificial intelligence are far from the world we know so well.

However, exhibiting only known phenomena in the course of scientific and commercial practice would lead to the public's aesthetic fatigue from overexposure. Aesthetic practice needs to create novel interpretations of familiar daily scenes to refresh the experience of the audience without challenging their understanding. For example, photography has

---

30 Google DeepDream was originally invented to help scientists and engineers visualize what deep neural networks "understand" of a given image. Lately, this algorithm has been used to imitate and learn about human artistic creation. Google expects DeepDream to create new forms of psychedelic abstract art.

always recorded the world that is familiar to us realistically because of its documentary nature. Nonetheless, some photographers produce work that is classed as artistic creation rather than pure documentation, since daily life seen through their lens carries new and unexpected meanings; for example, it may be redolent of a sense of alienation: the scene of deserted streets at three or four o'clock in the morning is in stark contrast to the hustle and bustle normally experienced at rush hour; the photograph of a fragment of sky encircled by skyscrapers taken from ground level symbolizes caged lives in modern society, but this perspective has long been ignored by citizens rushing past with their heads down. Our appreciation of music also embodies the sense of seeking unfamiliarity in the familiar world. When we listen to a piece of euphonious music, we find that novel compositions actually contain basic musical elements such as tune, timbre, and rhythm that are well known to us. The aesthetic feeling of auditory beauty generated by the music reaches its peak during its first iterations, as we develop a better understanding of the originally unfamiliar composition during this process. Later, we gradually lose interest in the music after several times or even several weeks of listening, depending on the fickleness of our affections. By that time, contemporary unknown has already grown too well-known—in other words, the construction of the music is no longer refreshing once we become too familiar with the work. This is one of the reasons why folk music, which is all the rage at one moment, eventually runs out of date.

In summary, the birth of beauty is based on a sense of familiarity and security, while almost any work of art demonstrates some degree of novelty and alienation. Aesthetic creation is the "dance with shackles on" that requires a good balance between comprehension and incomprehension. In other words, it should be incomprehensible at the moment of first encounter and eventually become intelligible after some effort. One of the reasons Nietzsche criticized the Romanticism represented by Wagner is that Romanticism is an artistic artefact created out of a scarcity rather than a surplus of intrinsic vitality. Nietzsche (1872/2017) considered, "due to its scarcity of intrinsic vitality, Romanticism preferred stimulating themes and the pursuit of exoticism, tyrannizing the nerves and giving narcotics and opium a dominant place in art" (p. 191). In fact, works of exoticism, such as *The Terrace of The Seraglio, Turandot,* and *Madame Butterfly,* were created in painting, music, and opera respectively during the Romantic period, in accordance with the idea that, "Life is more than just the muddles and compromises of the present. There are always poetry and distant places awaiting ahead" (Gao, 2017, n.p.). Nietzsche accurately criticizes the failure to capture the beauty of everyday life demonstrated by photography, for example, and the fanaticism for fresh stimulation, like exoticism, that is as addictive as opium to our senses. In the long run, artistic creation will not be able to rid itself of its addiction to novelty, and will eventually overbalance toward alienation rather than familiarity, absurdity rather than comprehension. Originally, beauty was more likely to be found in familiar environments than in distant places not yet understood. However, people today usually fail to grasp the extra intrinsic vitality of the familiar world in front of them, which reflects the lamentable fact that they are struggling and overwhelmed by practical activities and left with no strength to go beyond utilitarian pursuits to the superior and interest-free practice of artistic creation.

The last explanation for the flexibility (or the indescribable nature) of the standard aesthetic paradigm is that aesthetic presentations exhibit diversity from the fundamental and each type of beauty is the typical manifestation of each diverse possibility to the extreme. Compared to scientific and ethical endeavors that are subject to goals, such as seeking truth or welfare, artistic creations are free and diversified in expression because aesthetics is fundamentally beyond utilitarian pursuits. Aesthetic judgment is free of any particular interest except pure sensory pleasure. Therefore, possibilities that are too costly to test in actual scientific research or social mores/ethics can be discussed in the aesthetic practice of fiction. Both *Oedipus Rex*, in which the son kills the father and marries the mother, and *Hamlet*, in which the son vows vengeance against his uncle, feature homicide. Both *A Pair of Peacocks Southeast Fly*,[31] in which the protagonists hang themselves on a southeast bough, and *Romeo and Juliet*, in which the protagonists die rather than continue in life without the other, end in suicide. If these events happened in real life, ruthless laws and blind public opinion would punish and condemn them, regardless of the specific reasons for what happened, and would try to censor news of their actions for fear of imitators. It is only in fiction that there seem to be extenuating reasons for murder and suicide that are not necessarily regarded as cowardly and shameful. The art of tragedy discusses taboo social practices that are contrary to the will-to-live, establishing itself as a typical proof of the diversity of aesthetic presentation.

---

31   *A Pair of Peacocks Southeast Fly* is the first narrative poem in the history of Chinese literature. The poem tells the story of a couple who commits suicide for love when they are forced to separate, denouncing the ruthlessness of feudal rites.

Nevertheless, the art of tragedy presents us with extreme reactions against the will-to-live and creates the typical image of tragic heroes, since tragedy narrates its story out of sympathy for the losers rather than support for the winners and does not take an objectively neutral position. Our ordinary lives follow the rule of winner takes all, so that the establishment of social mores, the record of history, and the influence of public opinion are all dominated by the winner. On occasion, a rational social media outlet or an independent community breaks free from blind obedience and tries to deliver a fair assessment of the reasons behind violent incidents. It is most likely to draw a comment similar to what I've made in the epilgue *To the masses as well as to the mavericks*: "We would sympathize with some criminals sentenced to death about their experiences and even understand their situation... Would we pardon them? No, we would not, yet we would feel responsible for their crimes and their deaths... We should eliminate them, but what we need to wipe clean furthermore is the tragic world that breeds the darkness." The reason we express our understanding and show our sympathy in such a restrained and discreet manner is that we live in the real world ruled by winners where losers do not become heroes and nobody cares about the tragic experiences behind their failure. In fact, if we stand in a position of complete neutrality and objectivity, losers don't deserve the dignity of being sublimated into heroes in a tragedy. If it were not for the twisted plot of killing his father and marrying his mother, Oedipus would merely be an average person tricked by destiny; if it were not for the sinister deceit of his uncle Claudius, Hamlet would simply be a pawn who died in a power struggle with political opponents. Aside from the plot of dramas, we see ourselves stumbling and frustrated in the face of destiny's cruel joke or a powerful opponent in our lives, thus unconsciously projecting ourselves onto the protagonist of the story, but the tragedy is an artefact that is completely on the side of the loser and determined to sing the loser into a hero! Therefore, it emphasizes the brutality of the external environment to make the audience feel that the reasons behind their failure, which are treated as excuses when explained in everyday life, are eventually understood; it dwells on the inner struggles and unremitting efforts of the protagonist to fight their cruel environment in order to make the audience feel that their hard work, which has been ignored in real life ruled by consequentialism, is finally appreciated here. Only in tragedy can we recklessly sympathize with the protagonist and feel their endeavor as if we lived it. At the same time, we also lick our wounds together with the characters in the play, resolving the frustration we have experienced and achieving self-reconciliation.

A further reason why the art of tragedy is so intriguing is that the characters in the play have done something that we, who experience misfortune similar to theirs, want to do but dare not. Few would die for love like Romeo and Juliet, even if they faced the same unrequited love. Most would choose to live a life of regret from fear of death and family pressure. Few would take revenge with their own hand like Hamlet, even if they faced the same sworn enemies. Most would choose to suppress their rage and hand the matter over to judicial procedures. Hatred, killing, rage, recklessness… There are always some aspects of the id—animal natures undomesticated by civilization—that are subject to severe punishment if practiced in daily life but that can be thoroughly explored in literature. According to Freud, what Oedipus did unintentionally is exactly what each boy wishes in his subconscious: monopolize his mother's love and replace the father (for girls, to monopolize their fathers' love and replace the mothers).[32] Some believe that the birth of tragedy itself caters to an evil mentality in the frustrated public, behind which lies envy and a wish for others also to suffer misfortune. Just as sport has replaced war as a release for the excessive energy and aggressive violence inside humans, tragedy vents animal impulses and negative emotions that are rooted in human nature through fiction, thus reducing the frequency of actual atrocities and maintaining social stability.

As we can see, the aesthetic of tragedy is an ambiguous concept. Works of tragedy can be performed in forms as diverse as opera and movies. The splendid color of the stage and the heavenly sound of the chorus set off the noble image of the tragic hero, provoking pure visual and auditory pleasures in the audience. However, such pure sensory pleasures only account for the tip of the iceberg. The aesthetic of tragedy primarily relates to the psychological pleasure of venting. This includes the strong identification of the audience with the story, as if it were happening to themselves because of their similar experiences of misfortune, the resolution of frustration, the achievement of self-reconciliation through eulogizing and affirming the behavior of tragic heroes who are destined to fail, and the release of negative emotions (revenge, killing, rage, etc.) that spring from one's id but are restricted by social mores from being put into action.

---

32 Oedipus complex, in Freudian theory, is the complex set of emotions aroused in a young child by an unconscious sexual desire for the parent of the opposite sex and the wish to exclude the parent of the same sex. (The term was originally applied to boys, the equivalent in girls being called the Electra complex.)

Of course, there are more perspectives than solely the aesthetic from which one can appreciate tragedy. Some believe that the original intention of tragedy was, compared to the ending of a popular and mediocre comedy, the destruction of something valuable could teach the audience to better appreciate the glory of humanity that shone from the character and to acquire such goodness in order to succeed in real life, which is not as dramatic and cruel as the fictional environment. This is a typical utilitarian perspective: to watch the tragedy with a learning attitude in mind. As stated earlier, any masterpiece must possess a seamlessly integrated aesthetic exterior and profound interior, whose depth will sink into the viewers' minds naturally as they marvel at the gorgeous robe of the exterior. The entire process of message delivery takes place so effortlessly that it is not even noticed by the viewers themselves. From this perspective, if we are confident of the aesthetic value of tragedy, there is no need to hasten after quick success or overexert ourselves to gain an instant benefit during the process of appreciation.

The so-called social elites, on the other hand, approach tragedy with the purpose of experiencing the suffering of ordinary people. In their lives of constant success, the vicarious experience of failure stands for the unfamiliar in the familiar world and the unknown myth in the known story. They hope that such experiences will teach them new lessons about life and provoke refreshing sensory pleasure. However, unlike frustrated audience members, they cannot map their own experience onto the destiny of the hero in the tragedy; therefore, they fail to associate themselves with the story as if they experienced it in person. Tragedy is more like a gift to the suffering masses than a privilege to the upper class in this sense. If the suffering masses resist tragedy and indulge themselves constantly in comedy and burlesque, they risk losing the courage to reflect on their own failures and to reconcile themselves to their fate.

> A child has a caged bird, which it loves but thoughtlessly neglects. The bird pours out its song unheard and unheeded; but in time, hunger and thirst assail the creature, and its song grows plaintive and feeble and finally ceases—the bird dies. The child comes and is smitten to the heart with remorse: then, with bitter tears and lamentations, it calls its mates, and they bury the bird with elaborate pomp and the tenderest grief, without knowing, poor things, that it isn't children only who starve poets to death and then spend enough on their

funerals and monuments to have kept them alive and made them easy and comfortable. (Twain, 1899/2015, p. 140)

 Beauty is, in essence, the same as this bird—something pure and fragile that inhabits a corner of our mind. It pours out its song all day long, while most of the time, its singing is submerged by the noises of this utilitarian world. Do not let beauty die, and do not hold funerals for it. The goddess of beauty would never hold funerals. What we have buried is our overshadowed days, lost without beauty.

Renyuan Dong

Works Cited

Adler, M. J. (1997). *Aristotle for everybody.* New York: Simon & Schuster.

Ananthaswamy, A. (2013, January). Quantum shadows: The mystery of matter deepens. *New Scientist* 2 (2898): 36-39.

Austin, W. H. (1976). *The relevance of natural science to theology.* London: Macmillan.

Bei, D. (1990). *The August sleepwalker* [tr. Bonnie S. McDougall]. New York: New Direction Publishing.

Bentham, J., Ed. (1823). *An introduction to the principles of morals and legislation.* London: Macmillan.

Berkeley, G. (2003). *A treatise concerning the principles of human knowledge.* Mineola, TX: Dover Publications.

Brand, S. (1972). *Whole earth epilog; Volume 1180.* Menlo Park, CA: Porto Institute.

Burke, K. (1966). *Language as symbolic action: Essays on life, literature, and method.* Oakland, CA: University of California Press.

Carroll, L. (1993). *Through the looking-glass and what Alice found there.* Hertfordshire, UK: Wordsworth Editions Limited.

Castiglione, G. (1723-35). *Eight Horses* [Digital Image]. Beijing: The Palace Museum. Reprinted from Wikimedia Commons.

Confucius. (2015). *The analects.* Beijing: The Writers Publishing House.

Cosmides, L., & Tooby, J. (1997). Evolutionary psychology: A primer. *Center for Evolutionary Psychology.* Downloaded June 7, 2020 from https://www.cep.ucsb.edu/primer.html.

Cossell, L., Iacaruso, M. F., Muir, D. R., Houlton, R., Sader, E. N., Ko, H., Hofer, S. B., & Mrsic-Flogel, T. D. (2015, February). Functional organization of excitatory synaptic strength in primary visual cortex. *Nature* 518(7539): 399-403.

De Botton, A. (2004). *The consolations of philosophy* [tr. Zhong'jun Zi]. Shanghai: Shanghai Translation Publishing House. Original publication 2000 by Hamish Hamilton.

Einstein, A. (1905). Concerning a heuristic point of view toward the emission and transformation of light. *Annalen Physics* 17: 132-148.

Ent_evo.(2017, August 13). I think CRISPR embryo editing cannot achieve scenes like Gattaca or Beautiful New World. It cannot create a designed fetus. *Weibo.* Downloaded June 7, 2020 from https://www.weibo.com/

entevol?is_all=1&stat_date=201708&page=2#feedtop.

Feng, Y. L. (2008). *Preface to Sansong Pavilion*. Beijing: People's Publishing House.

Gao, X. S. (2017). *U can U BiBi* [talk show]. iQ1Y1.

Gibran, K. (2001). *The madman: His parables and poems*. Mineola, TX: Dover Publications.

Gibran, K. (1988). *Sand and foam: A book of aphorisms*. New York: Alfred Knopf.

Harari, Y. N. (2017). *Sapiens: A brief history of humankind* [tr. Jun'hong Lin]. Beijing: The Commercial Press.

Harman, G. (1973). *Thought*. Princeton, NJ: Princeton University Press.

Hegel, G. W. F. (2017). *Elements of the philosophy of right* [tr. Qi'tai Zhang]. Beijing: The Commercial Press.

Hume, D. (2012). *An enquiry concerning human understanding*. Mineola, TX: Dover Publications.

Ingres, J. (1814). *Grande odalisque* [Digital Image]. Paris: Louvre. Reprinted from *WikiArt*.

Ingres, J. (1856). *The source*. [Digital Image]. Paris: Musée d'Orsay. Reprinted from *WikiArt*.

Kant, I. (1981). *Grounding for the metaphysics of morals* [tr. James W Ellington]. London: Hackett.

Kramer, K. L. (1986). *World scriptures: An introduction to comparative religions*. Mahwah, NJ: Paulist Press.

Kumar, M. (2012). *Quantum: Einstein, Bohr, and the great debate about the nature of reality* [tr. Xin'zhou Bao]. Chongqing: Chongqing Press.

Luo, Z. Y. (2017). *U can U BiBi* [Talk Show]. iQIYI.

Ma, D. (2017). *U can U BiBi* [Talk Show]. iQIYI.

Maigne, J-Y., Chatellier, G., & Norlöff, H. (2004). Extra vertebrae in Ingres' La grande odalisque. *Journal of the Royal Society of Medicine* 97(7): 342-344.

Manet, E. (1866). *The fifer* [Digital Image]. Paris: Musée d'Orsay. Reprinted from *WikiArt*.

Mondrian, P. (1939-43). *Trafalgar Square* [Digital Image]. New York: Museum of Modern Art. Reprinted from *WikiArt*.

Nietzsche, F. W. (1997a). *Philosophical writings*. New York: The Continuum Publishing Company.

Nietzsche, F. W. (1997b). *Twilight of the idols* [tr. Richard Polt]. London: Hackett.

Nietzsche, F. W. (2017). *The birth of tragedy* [tr. Guo'ping Zhou]. Shanghai: Shanghai Translation Publishing House. Original publication 1872 by E. W. Fritzsch.

Nmlongyou. (2019, November 27). *The universe in the eyes of ants* [Video]. *TikTok*.

Rimsky-Korsakov, N. (2017). *Flight of the bumblebee.* Winona, MN: Santorella Publications. Original production 1899-1900, Solodovnikov Theatre, Moscow.

Running Mustang. (2010, December 31). Why do human have thoughts? What is human mind? *Sina Blog.* Downloaded June 7, 2020 from http://blog.sina.com.cn/s/blog_6b95c2fc0100o6s5.html.

Sagan, C. (2011). *The demon-haunted world: Science as a candle in the dark.* New York: The Random House Publishing Group.

Sartre, J-P. (2007). *Existentialism is a humanism* [tr. Carol Macomber]. New Haven, CT: Yale University Press. Original publication 1946 by Nagel.

Schopenhauer, A. (1974). *Parerga and paralipomena: Short philosophical essays*; *Vol. 2* [tr. Eric F. J. Payne]. Oxford, UK: Clarendon Press. Original publication 1851 by A. W. Hayn.

Schopenhauer, A. (2016). *The world as will and representation* [tr. David Carus, Richard E. Aquila]. London: Routledge. Original publication 1819 by Bibliographischen Institut & F. A. Brockhaus.

Seurat, G. (1884). *Sunday afternoon on the Island of La Grande* [Digital Image]. Chicago: Art Institute of Chicago. Reprinted from *WikiArt*.

Seurat, G. (1888). *Entrance to the Harbor* [Digital Image]. New York: Museum of Modern Art. Reprinted from *WikiArt*.

Solomon, R. C. (2008). *Big questions: A short introduction to philosophy* [tr. Bu'tian Zhang]. Guilin: Guangxi Normal University Press. Original publication 1982 by Cengage Learning.

Simard, S. (2016, August 30). *How trees talk to each other?* [TED Talk]. Downloaded June 7, 2020 from https://www.youtube.com/watch?v=Un2yBgIAxYs.

The Hubble Heritage Tea, NASA. (1999, June 3). *NGC 4414 galaxy* [Photograph]. Reprinted from *Wikimedia Commons*.

Thoma, M. (2015, December 7). *50 iterations of applying Deep Dream* [Digital Image]. Reprinted from *Wikimedia Commons*.

Tobi, E. W., Slieker, R. C., Stein, A. D., Suchiman, H. E., Slagboom, P. E., van Zwet, E. W., Heijmans, B. T., Lumey, L. H. (2015). Early gestation as the critical time-window for changes in the prenatal environment to affect the adult human blood methylome. *International Journal of Epidemiology* 44(4): 1211-23.

Twain, M. (2015). *Man that corrupted Hadleyburg and other stories.* Richmond, UK: Alma Books LTD. Original publication 1899 by Harper.

US National Cancer Institute's Serveillance, Epidemiology and End Results

(SEER) Program. (2019, March 17). *Neuron* [Digital Image]. Adapted from *Wikipedia Commons.*

van Beethoven, L. (1960). *Symphony No. 5 in C-minor.* London: Ernst Eulenburg. Original productioin 1807-1808, Theater an der Wien, Vienna.

Warman, M. (2011, May 17). Stephen Hawking tells Google "philosophy is dead." *The Telegraph.* Downloaded June 7, 2020 from https://www.telegraph.co.uk/technology/google/8520033/Stephen-Hawking-tells-Google-philosophy-is-dead.html.

Wenzel, C. H. (2008). *An introduction to Kant's Aesthetics: Core concepts and problems.* Hoboken, NJ: Blackwell Publishing.

Wittgenstein, L. (2014). *The tractatus according to its own form.* Morrisville, NC: Lulu Press.

Xiong, B. D. (2017, August 13). Why do I feel averse to the sound of fingernails scratching a blackboard? *Zhihu.* Downloaded January 20, 2020 from https://www.zhihu.com/question/63645245/answer/212732017.

Yi Xue Shou Zha. (2017, June 28). Cold knowledge: Fertility is the sacrifice for the individual survival at times. *Weibo.* Downloaded January 20, 2020 from https://www.weibo.com/ttarticle/p/show?id=2309404123765540791227.

Yu, J. Q., Takahashi, T., Hu, R. H., Gong, Z., Ma, W. J., Huang, Y. S., Chen, C. E., & Yan, X. Q. (2019, January). Creation of electron-positron pairs in photon-photon collisions driven by 10-PW laser pulses. *Physical Review Letters* 122(1): 014802.

Zhou, Q. (2003). *Introduction to college Chinese.* Kumming: Yuman Nationalities Publishing House.

Zhuangzi. (1989). *Lao Tzu, Zhuang Tzu, Lie Tzu.* Changsha: Yuelu Books.

Zhuangzi. (2001). *Teachings and sayings of Chuang Tzu* [tr. Herbert Allen Giles]. Mineola, TX: Dover Publications.

Zhu, G. Q. (2015). *Letters on beauty.* Shanghai: New Star Press.

Other Resources

Relevant publications

Carey, N. (2012). *The epigenetics revolution: How modern biology is rewriting our understanding of genetics, disease and inheritance.* London: Icon Books.

Putnam, H. (1981). *Reason, truth, and history.* Cambridge: Cambridge University Press.

Ma, X. G. (1995). *The study of Kant's Aesthetics.* Beijing: Beijing Normal University Press.

Recommended online courses

1 Philosophy, Science and Religion: Science and Philosophy

Various lecturers, University of Edinburgh

https://www.coursera.org/learn/philosophy-science-religion-1/home/welcome

2 Philosophy and the Sciences: Introduction to the Philosophy of Cognitive Sciences

Various lecturers, University of Edinburgh

https://www.coursera.org/learn/philosophy-cognitive-sciences/home/welcome

3 Modern Art & Ideas

Lecturer: Lisa Mazzola, The Museum of Modern Art

https://www.coursera.org/learn/modern-art-ideas/home/welcome

4 Understanding Einstein: The Special Theory of Relativity

Lecturer: Larry Randles Lagerstrom, Stanford University

https://www.coursera.org/learn/einstein-relativity/home/welcome

5 The Modern and the Postmodern

Lecturer: Michael S. Roth, Wesleyan University

https://www.coursera.org/learn/modern-postmodern-1/home/welcome

https://www.coursera.org/learn/modern-postmodern-2/home/welcome

MSI Press LLC

Publications in Religion and Philosophy

A Believer-in-Waiting's First Encounters with God (Mahlou)

A Guide to Bliss: Transforming Your Life through Mind Expansion (Tubali)

Blest Atheist (Mahlou)

Christmas at the Mission: A Cat's View of Catholic Beliefs and Customs (Sula)

Easter at the Mission: A Cat's Observation of the Paschal Mystery (Sula)

El Poder de lo Transpersonal (Ustman)

Everybody's Little Book of Everyday Prayers (MacGregor)

How to Argue with an Atheist: How to Win the Argument without Losing the Person (Brink)

How to Live from Your Heart (Hucknall)

Introductory Lectures on Religious Philosophy (Sabzevary)

Jesus Is Still Passing By (Easterling)/Study Guide edition also available

Joshuanism (Tosto)

Life after Losing a Child (Young & Romer)

Living in Blue Sky Mind: Basic Buddhist Teachings for a Happy Life (Diedrichs)

Of God, Rattlesnakes, and Okra (Easterling)

One Family: Indivisible (Greenebaum)

Overcoming the Odds (C. Leaver)

Passing On (Romer)

Puertas a la Eternidad (Ustman)

Rainstorm of Tomorrow (Dong)

Road Map to Power (Husain & Husain)

Saints I know (Sula)

Sula and the Franciscan Sisters (Sula)

Surviving Cancer, Healing People: One Cat's Story (Sula)

Tale of a Mission Cat (Sula)

The Seven Wisdoms of Life (Tubali)

www.ingramcontent.com/pod-product-compliance
Lightning Source LLC
Chambersburg PA
CBHW042132160426

43199CB00021B/2888